# *Galatians and 1 & 2 Thessalonians*

## BUILDING ON A SOLID FOUNDATION

BRIAN HARBOUR
GARY LONG
BOB DEFOOR

BAPTISTWAYPRESS®

Dallas, Texas

*Galatians and 1 & 2 Thessalonians: Building On a Solid Foundation—*
*BaptistWay Adult Bible Study Guide—Large Print*

BAPTISTWAY PRESS® Management Team
Executive Director, Baptist General Convention of Texas: Randel Everett
Director, Education/Discipleship Center: Chris Liebrum
Director, Bible Study/Discipleship: Phil Miller
Publisher, BAPTISTWAY PRESS®: Ross West

Cover and Interior Design and Production: Desktop Miracles, Inc.
Printing: Data Reproductions Corporation

First edition: September 2009
Large Print ISBN-13: 978-1-934731-35-2

# How to Make the Best Use of This Issue

Whether you're the teacher or a student—

1. Start early in the week before your class meets.

2. Overview the study. Review the table of contents and read the study introduction. Try to see how each lesson relates to the overall study.

3. Use your Bible to read and consider prayerfully the Scripture passages for the lesson. (You'll see that each writer has chosen a favorite translation for the lessons in this issue. You're free to use the Bible translation you prefer and compare it with the translation chosen for that unit, of course.)

4. After reading all the Scripture passages in your Bible, then read the writer's comments. The comments are intended to be an aid to your study of the Bible.

5. Read the small articles—"sidebars"—in each lesson. They are intended to provide additional, enrichment information and inspiration and to encourage thought and application.

6. Try to answer for yourself the questions included in each lesson. They're intended to encourage further

thought and application, and they can also be used in the class session itself.

If you're the teacher—

A. Do all of the things just mentioned, of course. As you begin the study with your class, be sure to find a way to help your class know the date on which each lesson will be studied. You might do this in one or more of the following ways:

- In the first session of the study, briefly overview the study by identifying with your class the date on which each lesson will be studied. Lead your class to write the date in the table of contents on page 9 and on the first page of each lesson.

- Make and post a chart that indicates the date on which each lesson will be studied.

- If all of your class has e-mail, send them an e-mail with the dates the lessons will be studied.

- Provide a bookmark with the lesson dates. You may want to include information about your church and then use the bookmark as an outreach tool, too. A model for a bookmark can be downloaded from www.baptistwaypress.org on the Resources for Adults page.

- Develop a sticker with the lesson dates, and place it on the table of contents or on the back cover.

B. Get a copy of the *Teaching Guide*, a companion piece to this *Study Guide*. The *Teaching Guide* contains additional Bible comments plus two teaching plans. The teaching plans in the *Teaching Guide* are intended to provide practical, easy-to-use teaching suggestions that will work in your class.

C. After you've studied the Bible passage, the lesson comments, and other material, use the teaching suggestions in the *Teaching Guide* to help you develop your plan for leading your class in studying each lesson.

D. You may want to get the additional adult Bible study comments—*Adult Online Bible Commentary*— by Dr. Jim Denison (president, The Center for Informed Faith, and theologian-in-residence, Baptist General Convention of Texas) that are available at www.baptistwaypress.org and can be downloaded free. An additional teaching plan plus teaching resource items are also available at www.baptistwaypress.org.

E. You also may want to get the enrichment teaching help that is provided on the internet by the *Baptist Standard* at www.baptiststandard.com. (Other class participants may find this information helpful, too.) Call 214–630–4571 to begin your subscription to the printed or electronic edition of the *Baptist Standard*.

F. Enjoy leading your class in discovering the meaning of the Scripture passages and in applying these passages to their lives.

# *Writers of This* Study Guide

**Brian Harbour** wrote unit one, lessons one through six, on Galatians. After serving as a pastor for more than forty years, Dr. Harbour retired from First Baptist Church, Richardson, Texas, to develop the Harbour Leadership Center and to establish a non-profit organization called SeminaryPLUS, which is devoted to coaching and encouraging pastors (see www.seminaryplus.org). He continues to serve on the Baylor Health Care System Board, as an adjunct professor at Dallas Baptist University, and as the Winfred Moore Visiting Professor in the Department of Religion at Baylor University.

**Gary Long** wrote unit two, lessons seven and eight, on Galatians. Gary serves First Baptist Church, Gaithersburg, Maryland, as pastor, and formerly served Willow Meadows Baptist Church, Houston, Texas. He has also served churches in North Carolina and Virginia. He keeps busy raising three kids with his wife, Traci. A native of North Carolina, he claims that his only troublesome vice is following the men's basketball team of the University of North Carolina. If he's on vacation, you'll likely find him on a sailboat in the Florida Keys.

**Bob DeFoor** of Harrodsburg, Kentucky, wrote lessons nine through thirteen on 1 and 2 Thessalonians. Dr. DeFoor served more than forty years as a pastor of churches in Kentucky and Georgia, serving the last twenty-eight prior to retirement as pastor of Harrodsburg Baptist Church. Both Bob and his wife Sandy are native Georgians, and they are graduates of Baylor University. Bob is a veteran writer of Sunday School lessons, and his Sunday School lessons have also been heard on radio for twenty-eight years. He and Sandy have three adult children and seven grandchildren.

# Galatians and 1 & 2 Thessalonians: Building On a Solid Foundation

DATE OF STUDY

## UNIT ONE

### *Only By Faith in Christ Jesus*

## UNIT TWO

## *The Gospel in Life*

*Introducing*

# GALATIANS: No Other Gospel

## A Hot Letter

Paul's Letter to the Galatians fits the definition of *a hot letter*. At points the words seem almost scorched onto the page. The letter was written in the heat of controversy and opposition, and it contains a forthright defense and compact presentation of the gospel that had grasped Paul's life so powerfully.

What triggered this white-hot letter? Paul was desperately concerned about the Galatian Christians. He put his concern pointedly, "I am astonished that you are so quickly deserting the one who called you by the grace of Christ and are turning to a different gospel" (Galatians 1:6).[1] One look at the bold expressions in this one sentence—"astonished," "deserting," "different gospel"—lets us know that Paul was dealing with what he considered to be a threat to the very gospel itself. In fact, the Greek word translated "different" in this verse means *another of a different kind.* Thus the Galatians were turning to a different kind of gospel, not just a gospel with a little bit of variation that could be tolerated.

## Where in the World Were the Galatians?

The Galatian Christians were located somewhere in what we call Asia Minor, in the area of modern Turkey. Two major locations have been proposed. One location is known as *South Galatia,* which indicates the area of the churches Paul established on his first missionary journey (Acts 13—14), the Roman province of Galatia. The other proposed location, *North Galatia,* refers to the area of northern Asia Minor that had been settled by ethnic Gauls, thus the name Galatia. The choice of the location of the Galatians affects to an extent the time in which Paul wrote the letter, but the message of Galatians is quite clear no matter the geographic location of the Galatians.

## Coming to a Fork in the Road

Whatever the location of the Galatian Christians, the main point is that they had come to a fork in the road. False teachers were encouraging them to take the wrong path. Paul was determined to make clear to the Galatian Christians that they must not do that. To take the path of the false teachers meant that the church would not simply be on a different path but on a path that was very wrong and that led to a disastrous destination.

The Letter to the Galatians is only six chapters long, but we will study it carefully and thoroughly in eight lessons. For all its brevity, Galatians is a key book in understanding the gospel, the life of the early church, and, indeed, all of the New Testament. Galatians goes to the heart of what the Christian life is all about, from the beginning onward.

Unit one of our study of the Letter to the Galatians consists of six lessons that consider the theme, "Only by Faith in Christ Jesus." These lessons deal with Galatians 1:1—5:1.

Unit two, "The Gospel in Life," treats the practical outworking in life of this tremendous truth of salvation by grace through faith. The two lessons of this unit deal with Galatians 5:2—6:18.

Today people seem either to think they don't need the gospel, good as they are, or to believe the gospel is about just being good enough or well-adjusted enough. To such a day, whatever the century, Galatians proclaims a powerful message. Let us be careful to pay attention to it as we study these lessons.

## UNIT ONE: ONLY BY FAITH IN CHRIST JESUS

| Lesson 1 | Only One Gospel | Galatians 1:1–10 |
| Lesson 2 | The Difference the Gospel Makes | Galatians 1:11–24 |
| Lesson 3 | United By the Gospel | Galatians 2:1–10 |
| Lesson 4 | One Table for God's Church | Galatians 2:11–21 |
| Lesson 5 | It's Faith All the Way | Galatians 3:1–18, 26–29 |
| Lesson 6 | Set Free to Be God's Children | Galatians 4:1–10; 5:1 |

## UNIT TWO: THE GOSPEL IN LIFE

| Lesson 7 | Walk By the Spirit | Galatians 5:13–26 |
| Lesson 8 | Life in a Good Church | Galatians 6:1–10, 14–16 |

Additional Resources for Studying Galatians[2]

Charles B. Cousar. *Galatians.* Interpretation: A Bible Commentary for Teaching and Preaching. Louisville, Kentucky: John Knox Press, 1982.

Richard B. Hays. "The Letter to the Galatians." *The New Interpreter's Bible.* Volume XI. Nashville, Tennessee: Abingdon Press, 2000.

Craig S. Keener. *IVP Bible Background Commentary: New Testament.* Downers Grove, Illinois: InterVarsity Press, 1993.

John William MacGorman. *"Galatians." The Broadman Bible Commentary.* Volume 11. Nashville, Tennessee: Broadman Press, 1971.

Leon Morris. *Galatians: Paul's Charter of Christian Freedom.* Downers Grove: InterVarsity Press, 1996.

A.T. Robertson. *Word Pictures in the New Testament.* Volume IV, The Epistles of Paul. Nashville, Tennessee: Broadman Press, 1931.

Curtis Vaughan. *Galatians: A Study Guide Commentary.* Grand Rapids: Zondervan, 1972.

## N O T E S

1. Unless otherwise indicated, all Scripture quotations in "Introducing Galatians: No Other Gospel" and the unit introductions and lessons 1–8 are from the New International Version.

2. Listing a book does not imply full agreement by the writers or BAPTISTWAY PRESS® with all of its comments.

# Only By Faith in Christ Jesus

One of the buzz words in American culture today is the word *paradigm*. This term comes from a transliteration of the Greek word meaning *model* or *pattern*. When a new paradigm replaces an older paradigm, commentators usually identify this as a *paradigm shift*. Paradigm shifts are shaking the very foundation of life in the twenty-first century.

Paradigm shifts mark radical changes in the world of education, for example. The old paradigm of education centered on time and place. The time was from age five through age eighteen. The place was the classroom. The new paradigm emphasizes lifelong learning, and the place is the world. The old paradigm was more theoretical and standardized. The new approach is more practical and customized.

The business world also knows about paradigm shifts. Business books line the shelves of our bookstores. In one way or another, every one of these books signals a shift in how business is conducted, how leaders relate, and how the organization operates. Each of these books envisions the new paradigms that will shape business in the early years of the twenty-first century.

Paradigm shifts also confront the church. As a pastor of the First Baptist Church in Richardson, Texas, during the last decade of the twentieth century and most of the first decade of the twenty-first century, new challenges and new expectations were my daily diet. These challenges ranged from the way the church made decisions, to new ways of being missional, to newer styles of worship, to changing schedules. We are going through a paradigm shift of major proportions in the churches.

Understanding paradigm shifts and how people react to them provides the setting for understanding Paul's Letter to the Galatians. When Paul met Christ on the Damascus road, he came to a totally different understanding of how a person relates to God. The gospel of Jesus Christ fleshes out that new paradigm. Paul explained and defended this paradigm shift in this letter to the Galatian Christians.[1]

## UNIT ONE: ONLY BY FAITH IN CHRIST JESUS

## NOTES

1. Unless otherwise indicated, all Scripture translations in unit 1, lessons 1–6, are from the New International Version.

LESSON ONE

*Only One Gospel*

## MAIN IDEA

Only the gospel of the grace of God in Christ is worthy of our commitment.

## QUESTION TO EXPLORE

At what point does acceptance of differing viewpoints turn into a denial of the gospel of Christ?

## STUDY AIM

To identify current substitutes for the gospel of the grace of God in Christ and describe how to respond in light of Paul's strong statements

## QUICK READ

Paul implored the Christians in the Galatian churches to remain committed to the simple gospel upon which the churches were established.

Most people understand the importance of being tolerant. After all, even Gamaliel called the Sanhedrin to be tolerant with these new followers of Jesus because this new movement might actually be from God (Acts 5:34–39). We too want to be tolerant. Nevertheless, we may worry that in being tolerant of other belief systems and the people who hold them we might eventually go too far and find ourselves on a slippery slope that leads us away from our own beliefs.

Paul accused the Galatian Christians of making that very mistake. Intolerance was not their problem. On the contrary, they were too tolerant. They were so receptive to the false teaching of those who were "trying to pervert the gospel of Christ" (Galatians 1:7) that they moved onto the slippery slope that led them away from the teaching about Jesus that Paul taught them earlier. Therefore, Paul wrote this incendiary epistle to call them back to the gospel of Jesus Christ.

## GALATIANS 1:1–10

1 Paul, an apostle—sent not from men nor by man, but by Jesus Christ and God the Father, who raised him from the dead— 2 and all the brothers with me,

To the churches in Galatia:

3 Grace and peace to you from God our Father and the Lord Jesus Christ, 4 who gave himself for our sins to rescue

us from the present evil age, according to the will of our God and Father, **5** to whom be glory for ever and ever. Amen.

**6** I am astonished that you are so quickly deserting the one who called you by the grace of Christ and are turning to a different gospel—**7** which is really no gospel at all. Evidently some people are throwing you into confusion and are trying to pervert the gospel of Christ. **8** But even if we or an angel from heaven should preach a gospel other than the one we preached to you, let him be eternally condemned! **9** As we have already said, so now I say again: If anybody is preaching to you a gospel other than what you accepted, let him be eternally condemned!

**10** Am I now trying to win the approval of men, or of God? Or am I trying to please men? If I were still trying to please men, I would not be a servant of Christ.

## Paul's Calling (1:1–2)

Few scholars question the Pauline authorship of the Letter to the Galatian churches. In fact, it is perhaps Paul's most personal letter. The section from 1:11 to 2:14 is clearly autobiographical. The references made and the statements given clearly point to the Apostle Paul.

The opening verses are more than just a standard way to open this correspondence to the Galatian Christians. Paul used these opening words to counter the charges of his enemies who questioned his calling. Paul's conviction that Jews and Gentiles alike can experience salvation by faith alone fueled their opposition. Even though the church affirmed Paul's position at the Jerusalem Council (Acts 15), the battle was not over with the decision of the council. These who wanted stricter requirements for becoming Christians were called Judaizers, and they continued their demand that circumcision and submission to the Jewish laws must be added to Paul's offer of grace. These Judaizers seemed to have special success among the churches of Galatia. So Paul wrote this Galatian letter to reprove this legalism and regain the Galatian churches for the gospel.

To support their case, these Judaizers made three specific charges against Paul. First, they charged that Paul was not an apostle. Paul answered this charge in Galatians 1 and 2. He affirmed that God called him (see Gal. 1:15). He affirmed further that the other apostles acknowledged his authority (see 2:7). Finally, he proved his worth by remaining firm at Antioch (see 2:11).

Second, Paul's opponents charged that his gospel was not the true gospel because he had no right to set aside the law of God. Paul answered this charge in chapters 3 and 4. Using the example of Abraham, he pointed out that God accounts a person righteous because of faith, not works. The gospel does not set aside the law but fulfills its original intention.

Finally, Paul's opponents claimed that Paul's gospel led to loose living. If people thought the law was no longer in effect, they would feel free to do whatever they wanted. Paul answered this charge in chapters 5 and 6. The compulsion of the Christian life, Paul affirmed, was not the law without but the Spirit within. Christian freedom is not freedom to do as we please but freedom to do as we ought. The Christian is one who walks in the Spirit, and the result is not immorality but righteous living.

These answers to the charges against him, given in their fullest form in the remainder of the letter, are given in capsule form in verse 1. There Paul identified himself as "an apostle—sent not from men nor by man, but by Jesus Christ and God the Father, who raised him from the dead."

## Paul's Conviction (1:3–5)

Paul's calling was rooted in a conviction about who Jesus is and what Jesus has done. Paul connected his opening expression of "grace and peace" to "God our Father and the Lord Jesus Christ" (1:3). By tying together the Father and the Son as the source of grace, Paul acknowledged the divine nature of Jesus. Jesus is not inferior to God in his person, and neither is Jesus secondary to God in his work. He stands as an equal to God the Father and is equally involved in the provision of salvation.

So what did Jesus do for us? First of all, Jesus took the initiative "to rescue us from the present evil age" (1:4). In that statement, we see the difference between Christianity and every other religious system in the world. Every other religious system is based on what humanity does to initiate God's love. The movement is always from humanity to God. In contrast, Christianity announces what God has done to make humanity right with him. The movement is from God to humanity. That difference marks the difference between legalism and grace and the difference between salvation by works and salvation by faith.

What else did Jesus do? Sometimes the New Testament speaks of Jesus ransoming us from the bondage of our slavery to sin (Mark 10:45). Sometimes the New Testament speaks of Jesus as giving himself as a sacrifice to cover our sins (Hebrews 9:11–12). Sometimes the New Testament speaks of Jesus as pleading our case before the heavenly Judge as our advocate (1 John 2:1). In this passage, Paul spoke of Jesus as our rescuer. Jesus came "to rescue us" (Gal. 1:4). We need to be rescued because we are a part of "the present evil age" (1:4).

Jesus rescues us, Paul affirmed, by giving himself for our sins (1:4). In that phrase we see both the measure and the motive of Jesus' sacrifice. Jesus was willing to give himself for us. He was motivated by our need. It is not the righteousness in our lives that inspired Jesus' unparalleled sacrifice of his perfect life. It is the *absence* of righteousness. Jesus gave himself "for our sins." Humankind has a problem from which we cannot extricate ourselves in a million lifetimes, and so Jesus did for us what we can never do for ourselves: Jesus gave himself "for our sins."

The final phrase in verse 4 has great significance. Jesus rescues us from this present evil age "according to the will of our God and Father." This final phrase reminds us that God is not a reluctant benefactor who has to be persuaded, almost against his will, to go along with the plan for humanity's salvation. The whole thing is God's idea. It is God's plan. This final phrase also affirms that Jesus is God's plan. He is not *one* of God's plans. He is not just *the best* of God's plans. Jesus *is* God's plan. It is the will of the Father that each of us should be rescued from this evil age through personal faith in Jesus Christ. That was Paul's conviction.

## Paul's Concern (1:6–10)

Paul's conviction gave birth to a concern that he immediately expressed to the Christians at Galatia, a concern that caused Paul to be "astonished" (1:6). The word "astonished" expresses amazement over something we do not understand and do not expect. Paul was "astonished" that the Galatians had turned so quickly from the gospel he preached (a gospel rooted in the conviction described in the previous section), to another gospel.

Paul used a play on words we usually miss in the English translation. Two Greek words can be translated "another." One, *heteron,* means another of a *different* kind. A second, *allos,* means another of the *same* kind. If I have an apple in one hand, and someone gives me a peach, I say: "Here is another piece of fruit—*heteron*—another of a *different kind*." If I have an apple in one hand and someone gives me another apple, I say, "Here is another piece of fruit—*allos*—another of the *same* kind. Both words appear in verses 6–7.[1] In essence, Paul concluded: *I am amazed you would so soon turn to another gospel of a different kind that is not another gospel of the same kind.* Any other gospel besides the one he preached was *heteron*—another gospel of a different kind—or in reality, not another gospel at all.

Paul recognized that some false teachers had incited the Galatians to turn from the true gospel (1:7). Paul leveled two charges against these false teachers. First, he accused them of disturbing the church. They were "throwing [the church] into confusion" (1:7). The Greek word means to *agitate or to stir up fear and uncertainty.* Second, Paul accused them of perverting the gospel (1:7). The Greek word means to *change something into something altogether different.*

Paul added this word of warning: "But even if we or an angel from heaven should preach a gospel other than the one we preached to you, let him be eternally condemned!" (1:9). Paul recommended a narrow-minded approach to the gospel that accepted only one gospel and that was the gospel contained in the conviction expressed in Galatians 1:3–5.

Paul called for the Galatian Christians to be narrow-minded about two important matters that are at the core of the gospel. First, they should be narrow-minded about *the One who saves us.* The New Testament from beginning to end is narrow-minded and intolerant on this point. As Peter put it in his sermon in Acts 4: "Salvation is found in no one else, for there is no other name under heaven given to men by which we must be saved" (Acts 4:12). If we are true to the New Testament, we must be narrow-minded about the One who saves us. We must also be narrow-minded about *the way Jesus saves us.* The New Testament from beginning to end is narrow-minded and intolerant on this point. Paul expressed this conviction like this in his Ephesian letter: "For it is by grace you have been saved, through faith—and this not from yourselves, it is the gift of God—not by works, so that no one can boast" (Ephesians 2:8–9). If we are true to the New Testament, we must be narrow-minded about the way Jesus saves us.

Tolerance, of course, has a place in life. We do not need to be like the person who was so narrow-minded he could look through a keyhole with both eyes at the same time. But on these two matters, we need to be as narrow-minded and intolerant as the New Testament. Only through Jesus is salvation available, and only through faith can we get in on it. That is the gospel. Any other message is not really the gospel at all.

Paul's unwavering support for this one gospel was not motivated by a desire for public approval. Instead, he was motivated by a desire to please God (Gal. 1:10). Life is a stage on which we act out our lives, and all choose their audience. Some choose humanity as their audience. Their primary pursuit is the plaudits of their peers. They are, as Paul called them, people "trying to please men" (1:10). Others choose God as their audience. Their foremost fascination is the favor of their Father. They are people who are seeking to *please God*. Paul put himself in the latter camp. He defended the gospel revealed in Jesus Christ because he believed this was what God had called him to do.

## Implications and Actions

We must remain faithful to the gospel of grace. Why? First, we must remain faithful to the gospel of grace, regardless of how much it is resisted, because legalists will continually oppose the free offer of grace. Too, we must remain faithful to the gospel of grace, regardless of how often it is distorted, because libertines will continually take advantage of the offer of grace to follow the passions of the flesh.

Resisting both legalism and libertinism and remaining faithful to the gospel of grace is also important because we are all doomed if we are counting on our own efforts to establish a right relationship with God. Our only hope is God's grace. Thank God, Paul persisted in his commitment to the gospel of grace. We must follow his example.

## GALATIA

What did Paul mean when he referred to "Galatia" (Gal. 1:2)? "Galatia" can be understood in one of two ways. The term can refer to the older kingdom of Galatia, or it can denote the Roman province of Galatia. This controversy of identity has led to two different theories concerning the recipients of Paul's letter. The *North Galatia* theory suggests Paul was writing to the churches in the independent kingdom of Galatia named for the Gauls who settled there in about the third century B.C. The *South Galatia* theory suggests Paul was writing to the churches in the Roman province of Galatia, to the south of the kingdom of Galatia. I believe the weight of evidence supports the South Galatian view. If this is correct, the churches Paul addressed in this letter were the churches in Lystra, Iconium, and Derbe, churches he established on his first missionary journey (Acts 14).

## A QUESTION

Luke tells of a young ruler who asked Jesus how he could inherit eternal life. When Jesus referred to the Ten Commandments, the young ruler responded, "All these I have kept since I was a boy" (Luke 18:21). Based on our text for this lesson, how would you respond to this young ruler's claim?

## QUESTIONS

1. What charges did Paul's enemies direct toward him?

2. Why was Paul upset with the Galatian Christians?

3. How do you see this passage applying to our churches today?

4. Why is legalism such an appealing option to us even today?

5. Can you think of some issue in the life of the church about which we have been too intolerant?

6. Can you think of some issue in the life of the church about which we have been too tolerant?

## NOTES

1. The New American Standard Bible translates Galatians 1:6a–7b, "for a different gospel, which is really not another." "Different" in 1:6 is *heteron*, and "another" in 1:7 is *allos*.

# LESSON TWO

# *The Difference the Gospel Makes*

## MAIN IDEA

Paul's experience with Christ led him to view life through the lens of the gospel rather than human tradition and live with boldness in response to God's gracious call.

## QUESTION TO EXPLORE

In what ways do we need to learn to view life through the lens of the gospel rather than human tradition and live with boldness in response to God's gracious call?

## STUDY AIM

To decide on areas in which I need to learn to view life through the lens of the gospel rather than human tradition and live with boldness in response to God's call

## QUICK READ

When Paul was called to preach the gospel of Jesus Christ to the Gentiles, this call, which came from God, totally transformed his life.

One of the courses I teach as a visiting professor at Baylor University in the Department of Religion is "Introduction to Ministry." The class members are students who believe they have been called into vocational ministry. A friend asked me about the purpose of the class. I responded, only half in jest, that the purpose of the class is to help the students discover whether they have been called to the ministry by God or their parents.

That is not an insignificant issue. I have known some parents who push their children into what in their eyes is an honored life choice. But their children might not have the gifts, the personality, or the spiritual depth to function in such a visible and high-pressure vocation. An essential element in serving well in such a vocation is sensing that one has been called by God.

Paul's critics accused him of calling himself into the ministry and then inventing the message that he claimed God gave him. In reality, his critics affirmed, Paul's message was simply an eclectic smorgasbord of ideas he picked up from other Christian leaders that he then reshaped into a slightly different form. In his letter to the Christians in the churches in Galatia, Paul clarified both his call and his message.

## GALATIANS 1:11–24

**11** I want you to know, brothers, that the gospel I preached is not something that man made up. **12** I did not receive it from any man, nor was I taught it; rather, I received it by revelation from Jesus Christ.

[13] For you have heard of my previous way of life in Judaism, how intensely I persecuted the church of God and tried to destroy it. [14] I was advancing in Judaism beyond many Jews of my own age and was extremely zealous for the traditions of my fathers. [15] But when God, who set me apart from birth and called me by his grace, was pleased [16] to reveal his Son in me so that I might preach him among the Gentiles, I did not consult any man, [17] nor did I go up to Jerusalem to see those who were apostles before I was, but I went immediately into Arabia and later returned to Damascus.

[18] Then after three years, I went up to Jerusalem to get acquainted with Peter and stayed with him fifteen days. [19] I saw none of the other apostles—only James, the Lord's brother. [20] I assure you before God that what I am writing you is no lie. [21] Later I went to Syria and Cilicia. [22] I was personally unknown to the churches of Judea that are in Christ. [23] They only heard the report: "The man who formerly persecuted us is now preaching the faith he once tried to destroy." [24] And they praised God because of me.

## The Source of the Gospel (1:11–12)

In our text, Paul began by boldly affirming that the gospel is no second-hand tale and neither was it created by human speculation. Instead, the gospel comes from God.

Now that is a stupendous claim to make, a claim that demands strong proof. Paul presented his own life as proof of the claims that this gospel came from God.

Paul had been the archrival of the church, doing everything in his power to destroy it. However, all of that dramatically changed on the Damascus road. After his encounter with God on the Damascus road, Paul's life spun off in a new direction. Now, instead of trying to destroy the church, he was committed to building the church up. How can we explain that dramatic change? Paul's answer is clear: only God can bring about that kind of change in a person's life. Paul's own life, then, proved that the gospel is a message sent from God.

How do we know today that the gospel of Jesus Christ is from God? With so many religions, how do we know that the revelation in Jesus Christ is of divine origin? As it was in Paul's day, so it is today: the proof is found in the arena of human life. When Christianity is tried, it works! When Jesus is believed in our heart, discerned in our head, obeyed and served in our home, and trusted and turned to in our hardships, we experience a new courage, a fresh sense of compassion, and an unshakeable contentment that we can find nowhere else.

## Before God's Call (1:13–16a)

God called Paul to communicate this gospel to the world. When God's call came to Paul, he was busy. However, unlike Gideon, who was busy advancing God's kingdom when God's call came to him (Judges 6), Paul was busy opposing God's kingdom. He wanted to "destroy it" (Galatians 1:13). The word "destroy" suggests a passionate desire to literally annihilate something. Paul's zealous persecution of the church put him in good standing with the religious leaders of Judaism, for they saw this Christian movement as a cult that needed to be stamped out. Thus Paul could say, "I was advancing in Judaism beyond many Jews of my own age" (Gal. 1:14).

But then, Paul discovered that this zealous persecution of the church put him in bad standing with God, for he was trying to destroy what God was trying to establish. Paul realized that the Christian movement was not a radical sect that needed to be eradicated but was in fact the community of God that needed to be established and nurtured.

When Paul highlighted his past zealous opposition of the church, he was not bragging about his past life. Instead, he was explaining that nothing in his past life qualified him to receive a call from God. His persecution of the church made him unworthy of God's calling. Too, his passion against the church made him impervious to any human invitation to become a spokesman for the church. Consequently, it should have been clear to everyone who knew him that his call came from God.

Paul elaborated on that call from God in the following verses. We see in Paul's discussion of his call a paradigm, a pattern, of how God calls people to serve him in every generation.

First, *the call came from God.* Paul traced everything about his conversion and call back to God. It was God who set him apart, God who called him, and God who revealed his Son to him. Paul's call came from God.

Second, *the call was rooted in God's grace.* Paul never lost the sense of amazement that God was willing to use someone like him to carry out his kingdom work. To the Ephesians, he admitted with breathless astonishment: "Although I am less than the least of all God's people, this grace was given me" (Ephesians 3:8).

Third, *the call* Paul became aware of on the Damascus road *had actually been issued at his birth.* Paul wrote that God "set me apart from birth" (Gal. 1:15). Rather than seeing this statement as a reference to predestination, we need to see it as another reminder that Paul's call did not come to him because of the gifts he brought to the table. At birth, Paul had not already proved himself to God. At birth, Paul had not already dazzled God by his brilliance. On the contrary, as a little baby Paul had no gifts to offer. Yet, while Paul was still an infant, before his gifts could be either discovered or exhibited, God had already designated Paul for this important assignment.

Fourth, *the focus of Paul's call was to preach Christ to the Gentiles.* God acknowledged that focus when God said to Ananias about Paul: "This man is my chosen instrument to carry my name before the Gentiles" (Acts 9:15). Paul confirmed this focus on many other occasions as well (Gal. 2:2; 2:8; Eph. 3:8; 1 Timothy 2:7).

## After God's Call (1:16b–20)

To reaffirm the divine source of his call, Paul reviewed his activities immediately after his conversion. When he arrived at Damascus, he claimed he "did not consult any man" (Gal. 1:16). Paul talked only to Ananias, who sought him out and delivered to him the instructions God had revealed to Ananias (Acts 9:17–18). Paul did not bring in a group of advisors, and neither did he visit with the apostles in Jerusalem. Instead, Paul withdrew to Arabia (Gal. 1:17). The Arabia to which Paul retreated was not identical with Saudi Arabia today, for the actual boundaries of Arabia in that day shifted with shifting political fortunes. But generally, Arabia refers to the area located between the Red Sea on the southwest and the Persian Gulf and the Euphrates River on the northeast.

What did Paul do in the Arabian Desert? What he did not do was seek out other people. Instead, he communed with God. He contemplated the miraculous change in his life and what it meant. He studied again the promises of the Old Testament that are fulfilled in Christ. In this time of personal communion with God, he prepared his heart for the work God had called him to do.

Only after shaping the understanding of his call in personal communion with God did Paul go to Jerusalem to connect his call with the work of the church (1:18). But even then, Paul explained, he did not gather input and suggestions from a wide range of people. Instead, he had some private time of discussion only with James. Even then, Paul added, this discussion with James was not an extended time of sharing but a brief period of dialogue that lasted a mere fifteen days. Paul did not go to Jerusalem to receive his mandate to preach or to receive his training to preach, for Acts 9:20 indicates that Paul had already been effectively preaching the gospel in Damascus. Paul's trip to Jerusalem was not for the purpose of having his ministry confirmed. God had already done that. He went to Jerusalem primarily to become acquainted with the other Christian leaders.

Apparently, the rumors spread by the Judaizers who followed Paul to the churches of Galatia claimed that Paul's stay in Jerusalem was an extended stay and that he received input from a large group in the Jerusalem church. Paul wrote the Letter to the Galatians to correct their misunderstanding. "I assure you before God that what I am writing you is no lie," Paul explained (1:20). Why was Paul so anxious for the Galatian Christians to hear the truth? Paul wanted to confirm that his message did not come by inspiration or imagination but by revelation. Both his call and his message came from God.

## Following God's Call (1:21–24)

What happened after Paul's fifteen-day stay in Jerusalem? Paul began to do what God had called him to do—to preach the gospel to the Gentiles. So he "went to Syria and Cilicia" (1:21). "Syria" is the region located between Palestine and Mesopotamia, roughly equal to the modern states of Syria and Lebanon. Damascus is the capital city of the province of Syria. Antioch, the city that replaced Jerusalem as the missionary base of the first-century church, is in Syria. Many Gentiles lived in Syria, the very ones to whom Paul had been called to address the gospel. "Cilicia" is the region just to the west of Syria, wrapped around the northeastern finger of the Mediterranean Sea. Tarsus—Paul's birthplace—is in Cilicia. In the area in which Paul was raised, many Gentiles lived. He would deliver the gospel message to them. Paul did not busy himself in discussions about what God called him to do. Instead, he busied himself actually doing what he was called to do—to preach the gospel to the Gentiles.

As he followed God's call, Paul's reputation spread in the churches of Judea, both those in the city of Jerusalem and others that had been formed by some of the Christians who left Jerusalem during the time of persecution after Stephen's death. Notice the spiritual location that Paul added to the geographical location of these churches. They were geographically located in "Judea." However, they were spiritually located "in Christ" (1:22).

The real contrast in this passage, however, is not the contrast between the geographical and spiritual address of the churches in Judea. The primary contrast Paul painted was between the attitude toward Paul reflected in the churches in Judea and the attitude toward him prevailing in the churches in Galatia. The churches in Judea heard the story of his dramatic conversion; they received reports of his powerful preaching; and, in Paul's own words, "they praised God because of me" (1:24). In contrast, in the churches of Galatia, the Judaizers stirred up distrust in Paul personally and doubt about Paul's message. So he wrote this letter to the churches in Galatia to defend both his call and his message.

## Implications and Actions

God has a call for everyone. God's call is to take precedence over our personal agenda and our personal desires. God's call is to have priority in our lives.

This does not mean we cannot choose to do something else with our lives, for we can. What it does mean is this: *we cannot choose to do something else with our lives and still be fulfilled, for fulfillment comes only when we discover what God has called us to do and then dedicate ourselves to it.* As God called Noah, Abraham, Nehemiah, and all the others in the Old Testament, and as God called Paul in the New Testament, God has called each of us with a particular call, and only as we give ourselves to that calling will we find a sense of joy, peace, and fulfillment.

## ROGER WILLIAMS

Roger Williams (about 1603–1683) was an English theologian and strong proponent of religious toleration and the separation of church and state. Associated with the Puritans in England, his ideas conflicted with the leaders of the church. Williams soon escaped to America, arriving in Boston in 1631 and then settling in Salem, Massachusetts, in 1633.

A year later, when the pastor of the local church died, Williams became acting pastor of the Salem church. Conflict immediately ensued. Critics in the church opposed both his calling and his message.

Williams moved to what is now Rhode Island. Eventually he established the first Baptist church in America, at Providence, Rhode Island, in 1638.

Like the Apostle Paul, Roger Williams was opposed by his critics. Also like the apostle, he followed his calling, even in the face of this strong opposition. In doing so, he helped to establish Baptists in America.[1]

## TO APPLY THIS LESSON TO YOUR LIFE

- Ask God to help you discover his calling in your life.

- Take time to inventory your spiritual gifts.

- Consider ways in which you can use those gifts to serve God's kingdom.

- Talk to others who are doing what you feel God is calling you to do.

- Look for open doors of ministry in which you can dedicate and develop your gifts.

## QUESTIONS

1. In what ways does living by the gospel enhance our lives?

2. Do you know someone whose life has been radically changed by Jesus Christ?

3. Have you sensed some specific ministries to which God has called you and for which God has uniquely gifted you?

4. Have you asked God to reveal the ministries in which he wants you to be involved?

5. Who are some of the people who have helped you understand God's calling in your life?

NOTES ——————————————————————————

1. Roger Williams. (2009). In *Encyclopædia Britannica*. Accessed March 17, 2009, from Encyclopædia Britannica Online: http://www.britannica.com/EBchecked/topic/644376/ Roger-Williams. See also William M. Pinson, Jr., *Baptists and Religious Liberty* (Dallas, Texas: BaptistWay Press, 2007), 49–50.

**FOCAL TEXT**

Galatians 2:1–10

**BACKGROUND**

Galatians 2:1–10

LESSON THREE

*United By the Gospel*

48

## MAIN IDEA

When our identity as Christians is defined by the gospel and not by culture, we find common ground for living and serving in unity.

## QUESTION TO EXPLORE

What would it take for all of us to get along?

## STUDY AIM

To identify elements in the encounter of Paul, Barnabas, and Titus with the Jerusalem leaders that would bring our Bible study group and our church closer together

## QUICK READ

The Christian leaders in Jerusalem agreed to collaborate in their efforts to share the message of the gospel with the world so they could reach all people, both Jews and Gentiles.

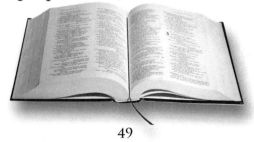

One of the most successful coaches in college football was the legendary Bear Bryant, who rose to fame during his years at the University of Alabama. Bryant once described his accomplishments this way: "I'm just a simple plow hand from Arkansas, but I have learned over the years how to hold a team together—how to lift some men up, how to calm others down, until finally they've got one heartbeat, together. . . ." He was able to get his players to work together as a team.

That is a singular accomplishment, to get people to work together as a team. It is essential to our effectiveness as we do kingdom work today.

We see a brilliant New Testament example of this kind of collaboration in our text for this lesson. The text shows that essential to the achievements of the first-century church was their ability to work together cooperatively as a team. Let's see how this came about.

## GALATIANS 2:1–10

[1] Fourteen years later I went up again to Jerusalem, this time with Barnabas. I took Titus along also. [2] I went in response to a revelation and set before them the gospel that I preach among the Gentiles. But I did this privately to those who seemed to be leaders, for fear that I was running or had run my race in vain. [3] Yet not even Titus, who was with me, was compelled to be circumcised, even though

he was a Greek. ⁴ This matter arose because some false brothers had infiltrated our ranks to spy on the freedom we have in Christ Jesus and to make us slaves. ⁵ We did not give in to them for a moment, so that the truth of the gospel might remain with you.

⁶ As for those who seemed to be important—whatever they were makes no difference to me; God does not judge by external appearance—those men added nothing to my message. ⁷ On the contrary, they saw that I had been entrusted with the task of preaching the gospel to the Gentiles, just as Peter had been to the Jews. ⁸ For God, who was at work in the ministry of Peter as an apostle to the Jews, was also at work in my ministry as an apostle to the Gentiles. ⁹ James, Peter and John, those reputed to be pillars, gave me and Barnabas the right hand of fellowship when they recognized the grace given to me. They agreed that we should go to the Gentiles, and they to the Jews. ¹⁰ All they asked was that we should continue to remember the poor, the very thing I was eager to do.

## Paul's Trip to Jerusalem (2:1–6)

In the opening verse of our text, Paul mentioned a trip he made to Jerusalem (Galatians 2:1). This verse raises three questions. The first question is this: Which trip to Jerusalem described in Acts parallels this trip mentioned here? Scholars are divided in their identification of this visit. Some identify this trip referenced in Galatians with what is generally known as Paul's famine visit to Jerusalem (Acts 11:27–30). On that occasion, Paul and Barnabas took an offering to Jerusalem to bring relief from the famine. However, this trip to Jerusalem referenced in Galatians focuses on the question of Jewish-Gentile relationships and fits more comfortably chronologically with Paul's trip to Jerusalem described in Acts 15. That chapter describes how Paul and others gathered in what came to be known as the Jerusalem Council. The question confronting the council was the same question Paul dealt with in this Galatian letter: What does a person have to do to become a Christian? Both the Jerusalem Council and Paul in his Galatian letter support the conclusion that salvation comes by faith alone.

This thought leads to a second question. What had Paul been doing during those fourteen years in the interval? The Book of Acts fills in some of the blanks for us, for Acts tells us that Paul preached in Tarsus and then went to Antioch to labor there with Barnabas (Acts 11:19–26). After a while, he and Barnabas went to Jerusalem on a relief mission (Acts 11:30). Then, with the blessing of the church at Antioch, they journeyed across Asia Minor on what we know as their first missionary trip (Acts 13). Now, after fourteen years of preaching the gospel and fulfilling his calling, Paul went to Jerusalem accompanied by Barnabas.

Question number three focuses on Paul's purpose. Why did he go to Jerusalem? Paul explained that he went to Jerusalem "in response to a revelation" (Gal. 2:2). We do not know what form this "revelation" to Paul actually took. God provided guidance to Paul in a variety of ways as we discover in the Book of Acts. On the Damascus road, God provided a revelation for Paul in a direct encounter with the resurrected Christ (Acts 9). In Acts 9:17, God provided a revelation for Paul through a man named Ananias. In Acts 16:9, God provided a revelation for Paul through a vision. In Acts 22:17–21, God provided a revelation for Paul through a "trance." We do not know what form the revelation took in this particular instance in Galatians. However, Paul made clear that God directed his coming and going. Consequently, God clearly directed this trip to Jerusalem. Whatever form God's revelation took, it compelled Paul to go to Jerusalem.

But why? Paul went to Jerusalem to "set before them the gospel that I preach among the Gentiles" (Gal. 2:2b). Two verses reveal why this mission was important, one in Acts 15 and the other in our text. Acts 15:1 identifies some individuals known as Judaizers who demanded that a person submit to the Jewish law before the person could become a Christian. In Galatians 2:4, Paul indicated that some of these Judaizers had infiltrated the churches in Galatia and were raising questions about the gospel and about Paul's message of grace. So Paul decided to go to Jerusalem to present his case.

We sense the seriousness of the issue in Paul's explanation that he presented his case "for fear that I was running or had run my race in vain" (Gal. 2:2c).If his gospel were not true—that is, if a person had to become a Jew before he could become a Christian—then Paul's time had been wasted. His fourteen years of ministry had accounted for nothing. He had run his race in vain. So he presented his gospel to the leaders in Jerusalem.

Paul referred in this text to two groups at Jerusalem. One group Paul identified as "pillars" of the church (2:9). He specifically named James, Peter, and John (2:9). James was a half-brother of Jesus. James did not believe in Jesus during Jesus' earthly ministry (John 7:1–5). After a resurrection appearance just to James (1 Corinthians 15:5–7), James believed and eventually became the leader of the early church in Jerusalem (Acts 15; 21:18). Peter was one of the Twelve; he eventually became the leader and spokesman for the disciples. John was one of the sons of Zebedee, also a member of the Twelve, with whom Jesus had a special relationship (John 21:20). These leaders of the church in Jerusalem concurred with Paul's position on salvation by faith alone. As a demonstration of their support for Paul's gospel, the leaders in Jerusalem accepted Titus as a full brother in Christ, even though he did not submit to the requirements of Jewish ritualism (Gal. 2:3).

Titus's status became a topic of discussion because of the other group in Jerusalem. Paul identified them as "false brothers" (2:4). Paul did not specifically identify these false brethren, but we can assume these are the same ones he identified in Galatians 1:6–9 who tried to pervert the

Galatian Christians' understanding of the gospel. Notice the derogatory language Paul used to address them. First, he labeled them as "false brothers." Then he accused them of infiltrating the ranks of the church. He further accused them of spying on the church. Finally, he claimed they wanted to make slaves of the believers there in Jerusalem. Yet, despite the attempt of these intruders to confuse the believers about the gospel, Paul assured his readers that he did not give in to their efforts.

Paul also pointed out that he was not unduly swayed by the Christian leaders in Jerusalem either. Paul's trip to Jerusalem to meet with the Christian leaders there might imply to some that Paul was submitting his message for approval to the Jerusalem leaders and that his message was in some sense shaped by them. Paul responded sharply in these verses by reminding his readers that the leaders in Jerusalem neither altered nor added to his message. He did not yield to any correction on their part (2:5), and neither did he allow them to add anything to his message (2:6). Instead, they concurred with the message Paul delivered to them.

## The Outcome of Paul's Trip (2:7–10)

If this trip to Jerusalem in our text is indeed the trip described in Acts 15, we can grasp the outcome of this trip by examining the narrative in Acts 15 concerning the Jerusalem Council. Three issues were at stake when Paul and the other Christian leaders came together at the Jerusalem Council.

Issue number one was *salvation.* What must a person do to be saved? The Jerusalem Council agreed that all can be saved by simple faith, Jews and Gentiles alike. James spoke for the Council when he said, "We believe it is through the grace of our Lord Jesus that we [the Jews] are saved, just as they [the Gentiles] are" (Acts 15:11). Because of that decision, Titus, a Gentile Christian who accompanied Paul on the trip, was not forced to be circumcised. The Jerusalem Council affirmed that a person is saved by simple faith.

Issue number two was *fellowship.* How can Jews and Gentiles relate to one another in table fellowship? To make eating together easier, the Council recommended some procedures for the Gentiles to follow, not in order to be saved but in order to enhance the fellowship between Jewish Christians and Gentile Christians. Luke spelled out these procedures in Acts 15:28–29, but Paul did not specifically refer to them in these first few verses of Galatians 2. However, the issue would resurface in the last part of Galatians 2 (see lesson 4).

Issue number three is *evangelism.* Paul concentrated on this issue in our text. How can the church reach all the people in the world who need to be reached with the gospel? Collaboration and not competition is the key. The leaders of the church endorsed this plan of collaboration. They freed

Paul to extend his efforts to evangelize the Gentiles. At the same time, Peter would continue to dedicate his energy to evangelize the Jews (Gal. 2:7), and God would use this collaborative effort to reach both groups (2:8).

Collaboration is also the key to reaching the world for Christ today. With a world to reach, we must replace *independent* thinking with *interdependent* thinking. Interdependent thinking will cause us to concentrate on *what* is right instead of *who* is right, on *cooperation* instead of *competition*, on what *we* can do instead of what *I* can do. No one style of evangelism, type of preaching, form of worship, or size of church can reach all the people who need to be reached. It takes all of us, using our distinct gifts, working cooperatively.

Paul added one condition at the end of this description of his visit to Jerusalem. While carrying out his God-given assignment to present the gospel to the Gentiles, Paul's Christian colleagues in Jerusalem asked him to remember the poor, something Paul was committed to doing (2:10).

Concern for the poor has been at the heart of Christianity from the beginning. Immediately after Pentecost, some of the new converts needed assistance. So the Bible tells us that the others pooled their resources to meet the need (Acts 2:43–45). This was not communism. It was Christianity in action taking unusual steps to meet urgent needs.

On more than one occasion, Paul collected offerings from those who had money to provide food and supplies for those who had none (Acts 11:30; 2 Cor. 8:1–9). This was not some radical view of wealth re-distribution. It was Christianity in action, taking unusual steps to meet urgent needs.

Christians of every generation have responded to the challenge to remember the poor; such a challenge also confronts us today. This command to "remember the poor" challenges us to open our eyes to people's needs. This command also reminds us that we are responsible to help meet those needs. It is not enough to feel sympathetic toward the poor and needy. We must also do something about the problem.

Evangelism and social ministry are not mutually exclusive activities. Churches do not have to choose one or the other. The church at its best in every generation has maintained a balance between evangelism and social ministry. Remembering the poor does not require us to forget about evangelism, and neither does evangelism force us to give up on social ministry. Instead, we must keep them in balance.

## Implications and Actions

This lesson reminds us that God gives different gifts for different callings. In today's churches we give a lot of attention to ordination and titles. But in the New Testament church, they gave their attention to gifts and callings.

Peter was gifted to preach the gospel to the Jews, and so the church confirmed him in that calling. Paul was gifted to preach the gospel to the Gentiles, and so the church confirmed him in that calling. We need to recognize that truth anew today and allow it to shape the way we do ministry.

There is no place in the church for the kind of discrimination that will deny these Spirit-endowed gifts and the calling of God in which those gifts are to be used. There is no place in the church for the kind of elitism that will evaluate some gifts as being unworthy and some callings as being unimportant. God has purposefully endowed believers with different gifts and has intentionally issued to Christians different callings. We need to recognize that truth. In fact, we need to celebrate it.

## GENTILES

The word *Gentiles* appears often in the Bible. The word literally means *the nations.* Originally, the word simply distinguished the Jews from every other nation. However, the term eventually took on the tone of disdain.

Yet in no age were the Gentiles excluded from sharing in the benefits conferred on the Jews if they were willing to enter into the covenant relationship with God. Some Gentiles were drawn to the monotheism and ethical standards of Judaism and became *God-fearing* Gentiles.

This term is used to describe Cornelius in Acts 10:2. When Paul referred to "Gentiles who worship God" in his sermon at Pisidian Antioch (Acts 13:16), he was referring to these *God-fearing* Gentiles. Other Gentiles went further and actually converted to Judaism, submitting to circumcision and following the Jewish legal requirements.

The initial promise to Abraham (Genesis 12:3) that included the Gentiles found fulfillment in the New Testament and particularly in the ministry of Paul. Paul was sent to preach among the Gentiles (Acts 9:15), and he proclaimed an equal opportunity of salvation for the Gentiles (Romans 1:16).

## TO APPLY THIS LESSON TO YOUR LIFE

- Acknowledge that God provides different gifts to different Christians.

- Recognize that these different gifts equip each of us to fulfill different callings.

- Discover your own specific gift or gifts.

- Develop and implement that gift or gifts for the cause of the kingdom.

- Confirm others in the use of their gifts.

## QUESTIONS

1. Why do you think the Judaizers opposed Paul's position on the gospel?

2. What are some of the dangers of the kind of collaboration illustrated in our lesson?

3. What was the significance of Titus in the incident described in our text?

4. What three issues faced the Jerusalem Council in Acts 15?

5. What implications does this lesson have for our churches today?

FOCAL TEXT
Galatians 2:11–21

BACKGROUND
Galatians 2:11–21

LESSON FOUR

*One Table for God's Church*

## MAIN IDEA

Truly receiving the gospel transforms our social relationships, leading us to accept all the people whom God accepts.

## QUESTION TO EXPLORE

What do we need to do to break down the barriers between ourselves and other Christians who seem very different from us in some way?

## STUDY AIM

To decide on ways I will open my heart wide to all of God's people

## QUICK READ

Paul called Peter to account because Peter's inconsistent response to the Gentiles suggested that some people are second-class citizens in the kingdom of God.

During various periods of Christian history, it has been especially difficult to remain faithful to the gospel. One of those periods was Germany during the 1930s. Nazism cast a dark shadow across Germany that affected every institution in German life including the church. Fear of punishment or a desire for political advancement led many German Christians to compromise the gospel. Others, however, stood firm in their exclusive allegiance to Christ, regardless of the consequences. Most of these who resisted Hitler's demand for total allegiance spent years in prison camps. Some of them, like Dietrich Bonhoeffer, lost their lives. One of the Christians who remained faithful throughout those difficult years was Martin Niemoeller. He survived his experience in the prison camp and emerged as one of the post-war Christian leaders of Germany.

The Apostle Paul demonstrated that same kind of consistent commitment to the gospel in the first century. He was like a compass needle that inevitably pointed in the direction of the gospel. Paul's unswerving fidelity to the gospel created conflict for him, not only with those outside the church, as we see in the Book of Acts, but also with those inside the church, as we shall see in this intriguing incident in our text.

## GALATIANS 2:11–21

---

**11** When Peter came to Antioch, I opposed him to his face, because he was clearly in the wrong. **12** Before certain men came from James, he used to eat with the Gentiles. But when they arrived, he began to draw back and separate himself from the Gentiles because he was afraid of those who belonged to the circumcision group. [13] The other Jews joined him in his hypocrisy, so that by their hypocrisy even Barnabas was led astray.

[14] When I saw that they were not acting in line with the truth of the gospel, I said to Peter in front of them all, "You are a Jew, yet you live like a Gentile and not like a Jew. How is it, then, that you force Gentiles to follow Jewish customs?

[15] "We who are Jews by birth and not 'Gentile sinners' [16] know that a man is not justified by observing the law, but by faith in Jesus Christ. So we, too, have put our faith in Christ Jesus that we may be justified by faith in Christ and not by observing the law, because by observing the law no one will be justified.

[17] "If, while we seek to be justified in Christ, it becomes evident that we ourselves are sinners, does that mean that Christ promotes sin? Absolutely not! [18] If I rebuild what I destroyed, I prove that I am a lawbreaker. [19] For through the law I died to the law so that I might live for God. [20] I have been crucified with Christ and I no longer live, but Christ lives in me. The life I live in the body, I live by faith in the Son of God, who loved me and gave himself for me. [21] I do not set aside the grace of God, for if righteousness could be gained through the law, Christ died for nothing!"

## The Problem (2:11–13)

Peter—or Cephas, as Paul called him in the Greek (and some English translations)—had come a long way as a Jew. Jews of the first century refused to accept the Gentiles or to have personal contact with them. Peter was a typical Jew in that respect—until God touched his heart. Through his experience with Cornelius, Peter learned that "God does not show favoritism but accepts men from every nation who fear him and do what is right" (Acts 10:34). Peter confirmed this opinion in his statement at the Jerusalem Council recorded in Acts 15. Peter told how the Gentiles had been welcomed to God, and then he concluded: "We believe it is through the grace of our Lord Jesus that we are saved, just as they are" (Acts 15:11).

Consequently, Peter moved past his Jewish exclusiveness and openly and freely associated with the Gentiles (Galatians 2:12). Peter's openness to the Gentiles was altered by the appearance of some fellow Jews from Jerusalem. When they arrived in Antioch, Peter withdrew from the common table he had shared with the Gentiles and held himself aloof from the Gentiles. Why? He was afraid of what these strict Jewish Christians from Jerusalem would think. By his action, Peter implied that he did not accept the Gentiles as equals before God. To anyone who observed him, Peter's action suggested that the gospel was not for everyone.

At this point, Paul called Peter on the carpet. Paul believed that Peter's actions threatened an important principle: the universality of the gospel. God had revealed to Paul a truth that gradually captured the heart of the first-century church: *the gospel is available to every person on the basis of faith and faith alone.* Whenever that principle was threatened, Paul confronted it. So when Peter separated himself from the Gentiles, Paul said: "I opposed him to his face" (Gal. 2:11), accusing Peter of hypocrisy (2:13).

To understand why Paul labeled Peter's actions as "hypocrisy," we need to remember Peter's life experiences. He was one of the inner circle of disciples with Jesus in all of the significant moments of Jesus' life. He witnessed Jesus accepting both Jew and Gentile (Matthew 8:11; Luke 4:16–30). He heard Jesus acknowledging the oneness in him of all believers (Luke 14:23; John 4:42). Peter knew from his experience with Jesus that Gentile and Jew alike are welcomed into the kingdom of God as equals.

Peter's experience with Cornelius (Acts 10) confirmed these earlier lessons learned from Jesus. While Peter was taking an afternoon nap one day, God reminded Peter in a threefold vision that nothing—or no one—God made is unclean. Then Peter went to the house of Cornelius—a Gentile—and shared a meal with him. He also saw the Holy Spirit come upon Cornelius and his family in the same way as with the Jewish believers. He had even given bold testimony before these very Jewish believers that

God was no respecter of persons (Acts 11:1–18). Peter knew better than he was acting at Antioch. That is why Paul labeled his action "hypocrisy."

But the most amazing part of the verse is not Peter's "hypocrisy." He had a history of vacillation. No, the most amazing part of the experience was Barnabas's defection (Gal. 2:13). Every other picture we have of Barnabas in the Book of Acts paints him in a positive light. Every mention of Barnabas shows him as a consistent encourager. Yet here in our text, because of the "hypocrisy" of Peter, even Barnabas became uncertain about his reaction to the Gentiles who had become Christians.

## The Principle (2:14–16)

In response to Peter's defection, Paul presented a principle that at first glance is difficult to grasp (2:14). Let us break down Paul's statement and examine it more closely. Peter was a Jew. There is no question about that. But what did Paul mean when he accused Peter of living like a Gentile? Perhaps Paul was referring to Peter's experience with Cornelius and his family when, traveling in company with the three Gentile men, Peter entered the Gentile home of Cornelius and ate with a Gentile family. Peter thus did things that only Gentiles would do. No self-respecting Jew would have done those things. In that sense, Peter lived like a Gentile. Now, however, he demanded of the other

Jewish Christians what he did not consistently follow himself, and Paul called him on it.

Paul set this principle of acceptance of both Jews and Gentiles in the context of a theological proposition: a person "is not justified by observing the law, but by faith in Jesus Christ" (2:15). Justification is the act of God by which God declares the believing sinner righteous before him. So Paul was dealing here with the basic religious question of life: *How is a person made right with God?*

All the answers ever given to that question can be summarized in two possibilities: we can be made right with God either by what we do or by what God does. Some people believe they can be made right with God by what they do—either by their obedience of some law or by their acquiescence to some religious requirement. The movement in this understanding of justification is from us to God. The idea then is that when we work hard enough or when we are good enough, then God will accept us. In Jesus' encounter with Nicodemus in the third chapter of the Gospel of John, Jesus dealt the deathblow to this understanding of salvation. Nicodemus was one of the most religious people of his day. Nicodemus was also one of the most righteous people of his day. If ever a person could have worked his way into God's favor, Nicodemus would have been that person. Yet Jesus told him, "I tell you the truth, no one can see the kingdom of God unless he is born again" (John 3:3).

On every page of the New Testament, the same message is clearly proclaimed. A person cannot be saved by obeying the law. A person cannot be saved by his or her works. A person cannot save himself or herself. Yet the idea persists. Why?

The idea persists in part because the idea is *reasonable*. We are rational people who have been taught, *You don't get something for nothing.* It is only reasonable to assume that we have to do something in order to gain God's affection.

The idea also persists because it is *reassuring.* Something about our ego makes us want to be able to take care of things ourselves. We do not like to admit our dependence on someone else, and neither do we like to admit our helplessness. So some people continue to insist that they can make themselves right with God by what they do.

The Christian gospel Paul presented to the Galatians counters this *works* theology with the affirmation that we are made right with God by what God has done in Jesus Christ. God has already done all that needs to be done for us to be made right with him. Our response—the response of faith—is simply to acknowledge that we cannot take care of the problem ourselves and then to accept the gift of life God offers us in Jesus Christ. We are justified "by faith in Jesus Christ" (Gal. 2:16).

## The Provision (2:17–21)

Paul then rooted this principle and this theological proclamation in Jesus' provision for those who believe in him.

Paul responded to one of the criticisms of the doctrine of justification by faith alone. The criticism goes something like this: *Your doctrine of justification by faith alone is a dangerous doctrine. By eliminating the law you also eliminate one's sense of moral responsibility. If people can be accounted righteous simply by believing that Christ died for them, then they will feel free to sin all they want to. Therefore, Jesus, with his plan of justification by faith alone, will actually be promoting sin.* Such a suggestion brought an immediate and intense response from Paul: "Absolutely not!" (2:17b).

The remainder of our text provides the reasons for that strong response. Paul turned the argument around on his critics by affirming that it was not the idea of justification by faith that promoted sin. Instead, it was the law itself that promoted sin (2:18). Paul anticipated here his later argument in his Roman epistle (Romans 7:7–8). Reestablishing the law as the basis for our relationship with God will not remove sin from our lives, and neither will it make us righteous before God. Instead, reestablishing the law as the basis for our relationship with God will actually stir up sin in us and thus confirm that we are sinners. This does not mean the law has no value. It does. Its value, though, is not in making us right with God but in driving us to Christ (Gal. 2:19).

Paul took the argument a step further. To say that the idea of justification by faith and not by law actually promotes sin and that we can solve this problem by restoring the law is not only a misunderstanding of the purpose of the law. It is also a misunderstanding of the work of Jesus in the life of the believer (2:20). When we are justified by faith alone, we are not alone, for we now have Jesus living in us. We have a new power through Jesus Christ. Of our own strength, we cannot produce the kind of performance God wants for us and expects of us. But Jesus gives us a new power that makes possible a new performance. We tap into this new power through the presence of Jesus Christ in our lives.

Paul concluded his argument by explaining that to support the idea that a person can be made right with God by his good work would be setting aside the grace of God through Jesus' death on the cross. That Paul would not do (2:21). Salvation by God's grace through faith is made possible by Jesus' death on the cross; that is the gospel Paul preached to the Galatians when he established the church there. Paul wrote this letter to challenge the Galatians to remain faithful to that gospel.

## Implications and Actions

Sometimes we have an idealistic picture of the first Christians and forget that even the greatest of saints had clay feet. I am thankful for the honesty of the Bible, for it shows us the dark side of all the men and women whom God used to move forward his kingdom work—

like Peter in this passage, like Paul in his conflict with Barnabas in Acts 15, and even like Barnabas, whom the early church nicknamed *Mr. Encourager* but who in our text succumbed to Peter's prejudicial view of the Gentiles.

This honest picture of the early Christians gives us renewed hope that God can use even people like us. This incident in our text also reminds us that every believer is important to God.

The differences that separate people in the world make no difference to God. That is why, when Peter's action signaled a difference in value between Gentile believers and Jewish believers, Paul immediately took his stand. We need more Christians today who, like Paul in our text, are willing to stand up for what is right, including in human relationships.

## THE CIRCUMCISION GROUP

When God made a covenant with Abraham, and through Abraham with the Hebrew people, he instituted the rite of circumcision as the sign of the covenant between him and Abraham. Not only the Hebrews but also any foreigners joining themselves to the Hebrew nation were to submit to the rite of circumcision (Gen. 17:12). The rite of circumcision marked the person's admission into the fellowship of the covenant people and secured for the circumcised ones, as members of the covenant, their share in the promises God made to the nation as a whole.

In the early history of the Christian church, those who opposed Paul's inclusion of all people in the gospel insisted that those who became Christians must be circumcised to mark their inclusion in the church. Paul referred to them in our text as the "circumcision group" (Gal. 2;12). The "circumcision group" is simply another name for *Judaizers*, the ones whom Paul confronted in his letter to the Galatian Christians.

## TO APPLY THIS LESSON TO YOUR LIFE

- Analyze the way you evaluate other people in the church.

- Note any inconsistencies in the way you treat fellow church members.

- Identify practices in the church that discriminate against certain members.

- Establish procedures that will eliminate this discrimination.

- Reach out to those in the church who are normally left out in the activities and ministries of the church.

## QUESTIONS

1. Why did Peter withdraw from the common table in Antioch and sit at the exclusive Jewish table?

2. What should Peter have learned from his earlier experience with Cornelius?

3. Why do you think Paul confronted Peter?

4. Can you recall an experience when someone stood up for a principle even though it created conflict within the church?

5. What distinctions do we make between people in the church today that reflect a prejudicial judgment similar to that reflected by Peter in our text?

**FOCAL TEXT**

Galatians 3:1–18, 26–29

**BACKGROUND**

Galatians 3:1–29

LESSON FIVE

*It's Faith All the Way*

## MAIN IDEA

Faith is the sole avenue by which we receive God's grace and are made right with God, from beginning to end.

## QUESTION TO EXPLORE

What act or ritual must be added to faith in order to be related rightly to God?

## STUDY AIM

To trace Paul's argument that faith is the sole avenue by which we are made right with God and to testify of what this truth means for my life

## QUICK READ

God's plan of justification by faith levels the ground in the church, for every person must come into a relationship with God in the very same way—through faith.

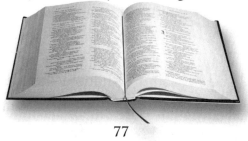

What is the most challenging question you have ever been asked?

One of the children who joined me at the front of the church for the children's story each Sunday morning once asked me, "How much does God weigh?" That is a challenging question.

A precocious young girl asked her father one night, "If a doctor gets sick and the doctor goes to the doctor, does the doctor doing the doctoring of the doctor doctor the doctor the way the doctor doing the doctoring wants to doctor or does the doctor doctor the doctor the way the doctor being doctored wants to be doctored?" That too is a challenging question.

Questions can stump us, as did the child's question about God's weight. Questions can stimulate our minds with their paradoxical possibilities, as in the question of the precocious little girl. Or, questions can cause us to rethink our position on a certain matter. Paul used questions in this latter sense in the opening verses of chapter 3 of his Galatian letter. Paul presented five questions that probed the minds of the Galatians and forced them to reconsider their abandonment of the gospel Paul preached while he was with them.

## GALATIANS 3:1–18, 26–29

<sup>1</sup>You foolish Galatians! Who has bewitched you? Before your very eyes Jesus Christ was clearly portrayed as

crucified. **2** I would like to learn just one thing from you: Did you receive the Spirit by observing the law, or by believing what you heard? **3** Are you so foolish? After beginning with the Spirit, are you now trying to attain your goal by human effort? **4** Have you suffered so much for nothing—if it really was for nothing? **5** Does God give you his Spirit and work miracles among you because you observe the law, or because you believe what you heard?

**6** Consider Abraham: "He believed God, and it was credited to him as righteousness." **7** Understand, then, that those who believe are children of Abraham. **8** The Scripture foresaw that God would justify the Gentiles by faith, and announced the gospel in advance to Abraham: "All nations will be blessed through you." **9** So those who have faith are blessed along with Abraham, the man of faith.

**10** All who rely on observing the law are under a curse, for it is written: "Cursed is everyone who does not continue to do everything written in the Book of the Law." **11** Clearly no one is justified before God by the law, because, "The righteous will live by faith." **12** The law is not based on faith; on the contrary, "The man who does these things will live by them." **13** Christ redeemed us from the curse of the law by becoming a curse for us, for it is written: "Cursed is everyone who is hung on a tree." **14** He redeemed us in order that the blessing given to Abraham might come to the Gentiles through Christ Jesus, so that by faith we might receive the promise of the Spirit.

**15** Brothers, let me take an example from everyday life. Just as no one can set aside or add to a human covenant that has been duly established, so it is in this case. **16** The promises were spoken to Abraham and to his seed. The Scripture does not say "and to seeds," meaning many people, but "and to your seed," meaning one person, who is Christ. **17** What I mean is this: The law, introduced 430 years later, does not set aside the covenant previously established by God and thus do away with the promise. **18** For if the inheritance depends on the law, then it no longer depends on a promise; but God in his grace gave it to Abraham through a promise.

•  •  •  •  •  •  •  •  •  •  •  •  •  •  •  •  •  •  •

**26** You are all sons of God through faith in Christ Jesus, **27** for all of you who were baptized into Christ have clothed yourselves with Christ. **28** There is neither Jew nor Greek, slave nor free, male nor female, for you are all one in Christ Jesus. **29** If you belong to Christ, then you are Abraham's seed, and heirs according to the promise.

## Questions About God's Plan (3:1–5)

Paul's opening question contains more the note of surprise and sadness than accusation. Paul was surprised that someone had so quickly "bewitched" the Galatian Christians (Galatians 3:1). "Bewitched" is not used literally to suggest a sorcerer had brought them under his spell. Instead, the word is used figuratively of the Judaizers who, with their words, brought the Galatians under their spell. To yield to such bewitchery was foolish, Paul declared, for the Galatian Christians were exchanging the gospel of Jesus Christ that brings freedom and security for a religion of rules that leads to slavery and misery.

Then Paul posed a question about the Holy Spirit. Did the Galatian Christians receive the Holy Spirit as a consequence of their following the law, or did the Holy Spirit come upon them in response to their faith? (Gal. 3:2). Paul knew that the answer was the second alternative. The first disciples did not earn the Spirit. The Spirit is a gift. The new believers at Pentecost did not earn the Spirit (Acts 2). The Spirit is a gift. Cornelius and his family did not earn the Spirit (Acts 10). The Spirit is a gift. Neither did the Galatians earn the Spirit. The Spirit is a gift. So the answer to this second question is clear: the Christians at Galatia did not receive the Spirit by observing the law. They received the Spirit by believing what they heard.

Paul's third question forced the Galatian Christians to recognize that their development as Christians, like their reception of the gospel in the beginning, was also driven by faith, not by obedience to the law (Gal. 3:3). If the Christians at Galatia received salvation by faith and if they received the Spirit by faith, why then were they being so foolish as to think that they could now complete the Christian life—that is, move toward spiritual maturity—by what they did instead of by faith?

The fourth question is somewhat misleading in the New International Version. Here Paul asked, "Have you suffered so much for nothing—if it really was for nothing?" (3:4). The context suggests a slightly different wording. Probably, Paul was asking: *Have you invested so much time and energy in the plan of justification by faith only to throw it all away now?* It would be like Billy Graham announcing that he really did not believe in the Bible any more. We would ask him, *Have you invested so much time and energy in the proclamation of the truth of the Bible only to throw it all away now?* Likewise, Paul asked the Christians at Galatia: *You have invested your entire Christian life in the idea of justification by faith alone. Why do you want to throw it all away?*

The fifth question relates to the provisions God has bestowed on the Galatian Christians as they lived their lives for Christ (3:5). Paul identified two things God had done for the Christians in the churches of Galatia. First of all, God gave them his Spirit. In addition, God worked miracles among them. Both of these provisions came not in response to their obedience to the law but in response to their faith. With Paul's probing, these Christians at Galatia were able to see that the source of their provisions and the basis for their power was not what they did but what God had done for them through Jesus Christ.

## A Historical Example of God's Plan (3:6–18)

Paul went all the way back to Abraham, to the beginning of God's covenant relationship with Israel, to find an illustration of the idea of justification by faith. Paul explained that God's original covenant with his people through Abraham, just like his new covenant through Christ, operated on the basis of faith. Quoting Genesis 15:6, Paul reminded the Galatian Christians that Abraham "believed" and that God "credited" it to him as righteousness (Gal. 3:6). Abraham did not work for that righteousness. He did not earn that righteousness. God credited it to him, because of his faith. Abraham was declared righteous before any meritorious deeds on his part, before he was circumcised in obedience to God's command, before he offered Isaac at God's request, and more than 400 years before the Mosaic Law was given. On the basis of Abraham's faith—not his obedience to the law—God declared that Abraham was in a right relationship with him.

So how could Paul's contemporaries identify with Abraham? Traditionally, the Jews believed physical descent from Abraham was sufficient. Paul presented a different answer. The true children of Abraham were not those who shared his blood but those who shared his faith (3:7). Because we can identify with Abraham by our faith and not by the blood flowing through our veins, this means that Gentiles as well as Jews can obtain righteousness. This inclusion of the Gentiles in God's covenant fulfills God's original promise in Genesis 12:3 when God told Abraham that all the nations of the world would be blessed through him.

Paul then compared the righteousness-by-faith plan he was presenting with the righteousness-by-works plan of the Judaizers (3:8–9). On the one hand, Paul affirmed that the righteousness-by-faith plan works. Those who turned to God in faith, Jews or Gentiles, were rightly related to God. It worked for Abraham, and it worked for both Jews and Gentiles in Paul's day. On the other hand, the law-works plan does not work. Those who followed the law in order to be rightly related to God—whether they were Jews or Gentiles—were doomed to failure, for no one can ever fulfill the law (3:10–11).

How then can a person be right with God? In both the old covenant through Abraham and the new covenant through Jesus, for both Jew and Gentile, and for both those in Abraham's day and those in Paul's day, the answer was the same: we are made right with God by our faith. The legalism of the Judaizers was not, then, just a variation of the gospel. It was instead a contradiction of the gospel (3:12). The law does not bring us the righteousness of God. Instead, the law puts us under the curse of God. So what can we do to get out from under the curse of the law? Nothing. That's the bad news. But the good news is that what we cannot do, God did for us, in Jesus Christ, through the cross. "Christ redeemed us from the curse of the law by becoming a curse for us" (3:13).

Paul mentioned two benefits that come to us when we believe (3:14). First, he mentioned "the blessing given to Abraham." This is a reference to Genesis 12:3, where God promised Abraham that he would be a blessing to "all peoples on earth." In other words, Jesus' death on the cross brings to fulfillment God's promise. Second, Paul mentioned "the promise of the Spirit." This is an allusion to Jesus' statement recorded in Acts 1:8. There Jesus promised the power of the Holy Spirit to the believers as they carried his witness to the world. In other words, Jesus' death on the cross empowers God's people.

Paul concluded his discussion of Abraham on a practical level by comparing the covenant God made with Abraham with an ordinary covenant Paul's contemporaries might make. The word "covenant" has a double reference. First of all, Paul used the word to describe an agreement between two human beings, such as a will. Suppose a person makes a will. When the person who made the will dies, the heirs cannot add to or subtract from the will. The conditions are already set. The promises are already made. They cannot be changed. Paul then used "covenant" to refer to the relationship between God and his people. If a human agreement between two parties cannot be changed when the party who made the agreement dies, it is much more true concerning the sacred agreement God made with Abraham (3:15–18).

## The Result of God's Plan (3:26–29)

God's plan results in a new paradigm for relating to each other, a paradigm Paul succinctly summarized in this final part of our text. Again, Paul made clear that this new context of relationships does not come because of what we do but because of what Jesus has done (3:26–27). We become a part of God's new family not because we follow the law, clean up our act, or are from the right family but because of what Jesus accomplished in his life, death, and resurrection. Paul spelled out the full ramifications of this paradigm shift in one of the most breathtaking verses in the Bible: Galatians 3:28.

Barriers have always existed between people. Paul identified three common barriers of his day in this verse: social barriers, ethnic barriers, and gender barriers. Paul was not saying that Jesus obliterated these differences. These differences are still real. Paul simply explained that with God these differences no longer make any difference. How much money a person has, what social status a person occupies, the color a person's skin is, or what a person's gender is—those things do not matter in whether or how God relates to the person, and neither should they to us as God's people.

This new paradigm for relationships does not ignore the barriers between people or deny that they exist. Instead, this paradigm calls for a different response to those barriers. In the kingdom of God, we are in a new relationship with one another, a relationship in which social, ethnic, or gender differences should be neither an advantage nor a disadvantage in our relationship with one another or in our service for God.

Paul applied this new paradigm to the specific problem that was fracturing the churches in Galatia, the assumption of the Judaizers that Gentile believers were somehow less than Jewish believers, or, to put it a slightly different way, that Jewish believers are somehow better than Gentile believers (3:29). Paul's conclusion is clear. The heirs of the promises of God to Abraham are not those who have Abraham's blood flowing through their veins but those who have been cleansed and redeemed by the blood of Jesus Christ.

## Implications and Actions

Every aspect of the Christian's life is governed by faith. The Christian life commences by faith. When Jesus ordered the rich ruler in Luke 18:18–22 to give away all he had and follow him, Jesus reminded him that his only hope of becoming a part of the family of God was to trust completely in God. That decision of faith is the key that opens the door to salvation.

The Christian life then continues by faith. Having opened the door to salvation by faith, we do not then take over the process of Christian development. Instead, we allow ourselves to be shaped by the Spirit of God who is in us. Paul pronounced this principle in Romans 12:1–2.

The Christian life also concludes by faith. The key that opens the door to heaven is not our resumé of achievements but the certification of our faith.

The Christian life commences, continues, and concludes by faith. That is the gospel Paul presented to the Galatian Christians. That is the gospel we still believe today.

## ABRAHAM

Abraham, the father of the Hebrew nation, was the son of Terah and, through Shem, a descendant of Noah (Genesis 11:10). Responding to God's call at the age of seventy-five (Gen. 12:4), Abraham moved from Ur of the Chaldees in Mesopotamia to the city of Haran in the extreme north of Palestine. God made a covenant with Moses (Gen. 12:1–3) that was expanded in later encounters (Gen. 15; 17).

Abraham demonstrated his less-than-perfect faith by taking his nephew Lot with him instead of leaving his father's household as God commanded him to do, by deserting the promised land for Egypt when threatened by opposing nations, by trying to pass off his wife Sarah as his sister when he feared for his life, and then by producing a child through his concubine when he became impatient about the child God promised him. Abraham's faith gradually matured as he laid the foundation for God's future dealings with Israel. The New Testament writers highlighted Abraham's trust in God (Rom. 4:18–22), his sacrificial faith (Hebrews 11:17–19), and his obedience (James 2:21–23).

## TO APPLY THIS LESSON TO YOUR LIFE

- Acknowledge God's preemptive work in every element of your Christian life.

- Remember that we obey Christ not *in order* to be saved but *because* we are saved.

- Yield your life daily to the shaping work of the Holy Spirit within you.

- While recognizing the reality of social, physical, and gender distinctions, resist using those distinctions to determine the value of people.

## QUESTIONS

1. About which element of the Christian life— the commencement, the continuation, or the conclusion—do we most often mistakenly interject the element of human achievement?

2. Why do you think Paul chose Abraham as an illustration of the principle of justification by faith alone?

3. Does the principle in Galatians 3:28 apply only to how a person becomes a Christian, or does it also apply to how we are to relate as Christians? Why do you make that conclusion?

4. Why do you think we persist in injecting human achievement into the dynamic of our relationship with God?

FOCAL TEXT
Galatians 4:1–10; 5:1

BACKGROUND
Galatians 4:1—5:1

LESSON SIX

# Set Free to Be God's Children

## MAIN IDEA

When we come to know God by faith, God frees us from whatever binds us to live fully as his children.

## QUESTION TO EXPLORE

To what extent have you accepted your freedom to live life fully as a child of God?

## STUDY AIM

To describe the life of being set free to be a child of God by faith in contrast to life otherwise

## QUICK READ

Paul reminded the Galatian Christians of their freedom in Christ and warned them to hold firm against all threats to that freedom.

She seemed to be a pitiful case. According to the newspaper account, this seventy-one-year-old woman, Bertha Adams, weighed only fifty pounds. She fed herself by begging door-to-door, and she wore salvage clothing from Salvation Army. She died of malnutrition in West Palm Beach, Florida, after spending the last few days of her life in a nursing home. When Bertha died, authorities discovered that she left behind a fortune of over one million dollars, including more than $800,000 in cash and several hundred shares of valuable stock that she stored in two safety deposit boxes. She had abundant resources at her disposal, but she chose instead to live beneath her privileges.

Many Christians are like Bertha Adams. With abundant spiritual resources at our disposal, many of us choose instead to live beneath our privileges, ignoring our freedom in Christ and instead living under self-imposed limitations or curtailing our activities for fear of criticism from others. Many of the Galatian Christians fell into the same trap, turning their backs on their freedom in Christ in favor of the limitations suggested by the Judaizing intruders. Paul challenged the Christians in Galatia to accept their freedom to live fully as children of God.

# GALATIANS 4:1–10

[1] What I am saying is that as long as the heir is a child, he is no different from a slave, although he owns the whole estate. [2] He is subject to guardians and trustees until the time set

by his father. **3** So also, when we were children, we were in slavery under the basic principles of the world. **4** But when the time had fully come, God sent his Son, born of a woman, born under law, **5** to redeem those under law, that we might receive the full rights of sons. **6** Because you are sons, God sent the Spirit of his Son into our hearts, the Spirit who calls out, "Abba, Father." **7** So you are no longer a slave, but a son; and since you are a son, God has made you also an heir.

**8** Formerly, when you did not know God, you were slaves to those who by nature are not gods. **9** But now that you know God—or rather are known by God—how is it that you are turning back to those weak and miserable principles? Do you wish to be enslaved by them all over again? **10** You are observing special days and months and seasons and years! **11** I fear for you, that somehow I have wasted my efforts on you.

# GALATIANS 5:1

**1** It is for freedom that Christ has set us free. Stand firm, then, and do not let yourselves be burdened again by a yoke of slavery.

## Before Christ Comes (4:1–3)

Life is full of passages through which we change from one status to another. Accompanying each change in status is a change of privileges. In the opening verses of Galatians 4, Paul described a remarkable change of status made possible through Jesus Christ. To understand Paul's claim, we need to put his statement in the context of Jewish family life.

In the ancient Jewish world, as long as a child was a minor, the child's status was the same as that of a slave. The child did not have freedom or privileges. Instead, the child was under the support and control of tutors and governors.

Paul used that situation as an analogy for the way God dealt with Israel in the time before Christ came. During the Old Testament period, Paul claimed, the Jews were like children. During their childhood, when they were not yet ready to relate to God in an adult way, God used the law and the ceremonies of the law to keep them in line. With Christ came a change in status, and with the change in status, a change of privileges.

Paul used this coming-of-age process to highlight the inferiority of people's status with God while the law was in effect, before Christ came. Before Christ came, still living under the law, Paul's contemporaries were no different from slaves. They had no freedom. Instead, they were in slavery to "the basic principles of the world" (Galatians 4:3).

Scholars have reached no consensus about what Paul had in mind when he referred to "the basic principles of the world" to which his contemporaries were enslaved. Perhaps Paul was referring to the basic principalities and powers that rule our world. In this case, Paul had in mind some kind of demonic bondage to these principalities and powers of the world. Or, maybe Paul was referring to the elementary teachings regarding rules and regulations, by means of which people attempted by their own efforts to achieve salvation. When Paul's Jewish contemporaries followed the rules and regulations of the law with the idea that they could therefore earn their salvation, the law became "basic principles" to which they were enslaved. Likewise, when his contemporary Gentiles observed the ordinances and regulations of their pagan religions with the conviction that this would bring them salvation, these "basic principles" enslaved them in a bondage from which they could not extricate themselves. So Paul used this coming-of-age process in the culture of his day to explain the Galatians'—and our—condition before Christ came.

## After Christ Comes (4:4–7)

After Christ came, however, the whole situation changed. Jesus appeared on the scene "when the time had fully come" (Gal. 4:4) or in the graphic language of the King James Bible, it happened in "the fullness of the time."

What does that mean? Perhaps this is a reference to *the Roman peace* that extended over most of the civilized earth, enabling worldwide travel and commerce that earlier had been impossible. Or maybe this is a reference to *the great Roman road system* that linked the empire of the Caesars. Or maybe this is a reference to *the all-pervasive language of the Greeks* that made communication possible on a wider scale than the world had ever known before. Or maybe this is a reference *to the presence of Jewish synagogues* in many places, which gave the Christian missionaries a place to contact both the Jewish believers and the Gentile proselytes. Or maybe this is a reference to *the spiritual condition of the world*, a world that had sunk into a moral abyss so low that even the pagans cried out against it, a world in which spiritual hunger was everywhere evident. All of these factors contributed to making the first-century world the appropriate time for God to break into history in Jesus Christ. When the time is just right, God acts.

At that time, God sent Jesus "born of a woman" (4:4). Some have suggested that Paul used that phrase to assert the virgin birth of Jesus. They translate this phrase to say: *born of a woman without the aid of a human father.* While Jesus' virgin birth is clearly stated in Matthew 1:18–25 and Luke 1:34–35, that is probably not what Paul was saying here. In this statement in Galatians 4:4, Paul affirmed the humanity of Jesus. Jesus is the Son of God—that is the divine element. But Jesus was born of a woman—that is the human element. Both elements are essential for a proper understanding of who Jesus is. Both were required if Jesus was to obtain salvation for us. If he was not human, his act of salvation would have no effect on us. If Jesus was not divine, he would not have been able to accomplish our salvation. Both Jesus' humanity and Jesus' divinity were essential for him to achieve our salvation. The accompanying phrase in verse 4—"born under law"—further identifies Jesus with those whom he has come to save.

Paul's emphasis in this verse is not on Jesus' *identity* with humanity, however, but on Jesus' *provision* for humanity. He was "born under law," but he was not under sin. Instead, Jesus fully followed the law as no other person has ever done. Consequently, Jesus is able to redeem those of us who are under the law and restore us to our full privilege as children of God (4:5).

Jesus' provision changes our relationship with God. No longer are we estranged from God. Instead, we can address God once more as "Father" (4:6). Jesus' provision also changes our status before God. No longer are we slaves, devoid of privileges. Instead, now we have become children of God, heirs to all God's promises (4:7). What a marvelous transformation Jesus brings about in our lives when he adopts us into God's forever family.

## A Word of Warning (4:8–10)

Paul compared the spiritual condition of the Galatian Christians before they came to Christ with their condition afterward. What was their condition before they came to

Christ? They were "slaves to those who by nature are not gods" (4:8). "Those who by nature are not gods" were the idols the Galatians worshiped before they came to know the true God through Jesus Christ.

While visiting in Thailand several years ago, I saw a small temple that contained sacrifices made to dozens of idols. It was almost as if the people were trying to cover all the bases. That was what the Galatians were like before they came to Christ. They worshiped many different gods because they did not know any better. When Christ came, their condition changed. Now they knew better. Now, through Christ, they had come to know the true God.

That is why Paul was appalled that these Christians in the Galatian churches were going back to their old ways. They were turning back to two things from which they had been rescued—ignorance and enslavement. This was not a new error to which they were turning. Jesus had saved them from that. Jesus had shown them the true way. Jesus had connected them with the true God. Yet, now they were turning back to the same kind of slavery, merely exchanging their slavery to the pagan rituals for slavery to the rituals of Jewish legalism.

Specifically, Paul chided them for "observing special days and months and seasons and years" (4:10). Amazingly, Paul the Jew not only opposed slavishly submitting to these Jewish rituals, but he also regarded them in exactly the same light as the pagan festivals. They were all activities controlled by and interacting with demonic spirits that resulted in slavery.

## A Challenge to Claim Their Freedom (5:1)

In contrast to this loss of freedom that comes from yielding to the requirements of Jewish legalism, Paul highlighted again the freedom that is available in Christ. This freedom is both a freedom *from* and a freedom *for*. We are freed *from* the curse of the law. The law pronounces a curse on all people who strive—unsuccessfully—to achieve righteousness by their own efforts. Christ rescued us from that curse by becoming the curse for us (Gal. 3:13). We are also freed *for* a life for God. What we could not do on our own, we now are enabled to do by the gift of the Spirit given to those who are in Christ. Christ set us free to be who we were redeemed to be (Romans 8:3–4).

But freedom is a frightening thing at times, and the responsibility of freedom is hard to bear. How easy it is to slip back into legalism. This was the issue facing the Galatian Christians. So Paul challenged them to stand firm in their freedom. The Judaizers tempted the Galatian Christians to go back to the slavery of the legal system from which they had been rescued. So Paul wrote, *Don't do it*. "Stand firm." The Judaizers laid a trap for the Gentile Christians, to catch them in a legalism that would rob them of their freedom. So Paul wrote, "Do not let yourselves be burdened again by a yoke of slavery." Christ set the Galatians free. Why should they want to go back to the prison of legalism?

We do not have to look far to realize that many Christians today are falling into the same trap as the Galatian Christians and consequently are living beneath their privileges. Instead of experiencing joy, many Christians are sad. Instead of having a deep sense of peace, many Christians are stressed out. Instead of being energized by the power of God, many Christians are ineffective. Instead of exhibiting confidence, many Christians are paralyzed with a feeling of inferiority. Many Christians are living beneath their privileges.

Through Christ, we have been elevated to a new status where we have available to us all the resources and riches of God. When we appropriate those resources into our lives, we will experience the joy, peace, power, and confidence God intended us to have as his children.

## Implications and Actions

I remember a commercial boxing star Sugar Ray Leonard made a few years back at the height of his popularity. He was advertising a soft drink. As he took a gulp of this drink, several children watched him in awe from a distance. But one child ran right up to the champ and hugged him. We heard no awe in this child's voice, only admiration and love. What was the difference between the group of children who watched Sugar Ray from a distance and the one boy who ran up to him and hugged him? The boy who ran up to him and hugged him was his son. The children at a distance said, *That's the champ.* But the boy up close said, *No, it's my dad.*

As children of God, we have the privilege of seeing God up close rather than at a distance. We can approach God not merely in awe but with affection because we have been adopted as God's children. We *are* God's children. We have been given the privilege of access to God. We need to quit living beneath our privileges.

## FREEDOM

Although a person has some freedom of choice in daily affairs, no person is completely free. Each of us is subject to drought, war, and other calamities. The decisions of others affect our lives. Too, we are all surrounded by people more powerful than we are and circumstances we cannot completely control. In addition, our inner selves are controlled by the pull of sin that prevents us from doing what we really want to do (Rom. 7:15–24). However, what we cannot achieve on our own is made available through Christ (Rom. 7:25). What we cannot accomplish in our own power we can accomplish through the power of Christ at work within us (Phil. 4:13).

This is the "freedom" (Gal. 5:1) Paul talked about in our text, and it is a freedom that comes from Christ. Jesus Christ liberates us to become what God created us to be and frees us to do what Christ has redeemed us to do.

## TO APPLY THIS LESSON TO YOUR LIFE

- Evaluate your life in light of the privileges of the Christian life suggested in Galatians 4:1–10 (see also Rom. 8).

- Encourage others to live up to their privileges as Christians.

- Refrain from insisting that others follow your understanding of the Christian life.

- Resist anyone or anything that limits your rightful freedom as a child of God.

## QUESTIONS

1. In what ways do you think Christians live beneath their privileges today?

2. What were some of the factors that made the first-century world suitable for the coming of Christ?

3. What is the significance of the descriptive phrase that Jesus was "born of a woman" (Gal. 4:4)?

4. Why is it important to include both Jesus' humanity and his divinity when understanding his work as the world's Savior?

5. What are some ideas prevalent in the church today
   that tend to limit our freedom in Christ?

# The Gospel in Life

Unit two, "The Gospel in Life," treats the practical outworking in life and in Christian community of the tremendous truth of salvation by grace through faith. The two lessons of this unit deal with Galatians 5:2—6:18.

Life has its challenges and joys. It can be gritty and earthy, as well as holy and wondrous. The lessons "Walk By the Spirit" (Galatians 5:13–26) and "Life in a Good Church" (Gal. 6:1–10, 14–16) explore Paul's thinking about the practical side of how the gospel is to be expressed in life, including life in Christian community.

Lesson seven deals with how to live in God's Spirit and avoid being trapped in legalism. Throughout the Letter to the Galatians, Paul encouraged walking by the Spirit. For Christians to walk by the Spirit, the implications of our freedom in Christ have to be considered. Our freedom is not granted so we can wrangle our own way forward but rather that we might bear spiritual fruit to benefit the lives of others around us. Paul framed clearly for us the emphasis that we are to strive hard toward loving neighbor as self.

Lesson eight treats various aspects of what living in Christian community means. The Scriptures in this lesson speak of sharing burdens, cares, the life of worship, and the tasks of ministry. They also speak of one of the most difficult matters in all of church life—how to relate to members who have sinned—as well as offer caution about how one lives and evaluates one's own Christian life. These challenging passages call us to reflect deeply on our discipleship as well as on how we can convey grace to one another.[1]

## UNIT TWO: THE GOSPEL IN LIFE

Lesson 7    Walk By the Spirit                Galatians 5:13–26
Lesson 8    Life in a Good Church             Galatians 6:1–10, 14–16

## NOTES

1. Unless otherwise indicated, all Scriptures translations in unit 2, lessons 7–8, are from the New International Version.

**FOCAL TEXT**

Galatians 5:13–26

**BACKGROUND**

Galatians 5:2–26

LESSON SEVEN

# *Walk By the Spirit*

## MAIN IDEA

Living by God's Spirit rather than keeping the law enables God's people to love others and show in their lives the fruit of the Spirit, not the works of the flesh.

## QUESTION TO EXPLORE

Is living by God's Spirit rather than keeping the law sufficient to keep us on the right track in life?

## STUDY AIM

To contrast life in the Spirit to fulfilling the desires of the flesh and evaluate my life by the qualities of life in the Spirit

## QUICK READ

We are free to live by the Spirit, rather than by the law. Spirit-guided living produces good fruit in the lives of believers—fruit for sharing with others.

My first car, a gift from my father, brought me all kinds of new freedoms. I could go out on Friday night, drive myself to school, or go to a friend's house to study. I learned quickly, though, that the car also represented a great deal of responsibility. It could transport me to fun events, but it also transported me to my job. There I earned money to pay the insurance, gas, and maintenance on my car. My driver's education instructor taught me that my car also came with a lethal power if I drove irresponsibly.

Paul taught something similar about freedom and responsibility in Galatians 5:13–26. We followers of Christ are called to be free from the law, he argued. He also said that with our freedom in Christ comes great responsibility, summed up in the single command, "Love your neighbor as yourself" (Galatians 5:14).

Many Christians, perhaps particularly those new in the faith, are tempted to fall into the trap of thinking, *I have God's grace, and so I'll live however I want to live.* But as I matured in my understanding of responsibility concerning my first car, believers must also mature in their faith and recognize that God's grace, which grants us freedom from the law, does not give a signed blank check to sin. The responsibility of grace is to "serve one another in love" (Gal. 5:13).

# GALATIANS 5:13–26

**13** You, my brothers, were called to be free. But do not use your freedom to indulge the sinful nature ; rather, serve one another in love. **14** The entire law is summed up in a single command: "Love your neighbor as yourself." **15** If you keep on biting and devouring each other, watch out or you will be destroyed by each other.

**16** So I say, live by the Spirit, and you will not gratify the desires of the sinful nature. **17** For the sinful nature desires what is contrary to the Spirit, and the Spirit what is contrary to the sinful nature. They are in conflict with each other, so that you do not do what you want. **18** But if you are led by the Spirit, you are not under law.

**19** The acts of the sinful nature are obvious: sexual immorality, impurity and debauchery; **20** idolatry and witchcraft; hatred, discord, jealousy, fits of rage, selfish ambition, dissensions, factions **21** and envy; drunkenness, orgies, and the like. I warn you, as I did before, that those who live like this will not inherit the kingdom of God.

**22** But the fruit of the Spirit is love, joy, peace, patience, kindness, goodness, faithfulness, **23** gentleness and self-control. Against such things there is no law. **24** Those who belong to Christ Jesus have crucified the sinful nature with its passions and desires. **25** Since we live by the Spirit, let us keep in step with the Spirit. **26** Let us not become conceited, provoking and envying each other.

## Freedom and Love (5:13–15)

Paul taught love of neighbor as the responsibility paired with our freedom in Christ. The love of neighbor as self is a calling to a higher righteousness, a higher set of standards for living. Paul essentially recognized that, yes, we are prone to sin. No matter how hard we try, our sinful nature will forever be at work in us, tempting us to do wrong things as we did before we knew Christ.

But Paul also recognized that even though sin is unavoidable, we now *know better.* Perhaps you've had to confront someone with those words, *But you knew better than to do this!* It could be a child or teenager who has been repeatedly warned but still chooses wrong. Or perhaps the shoe is on the other foot, an employer has warned you about job performance, and you still chose to be slack. You *know better* but still proceed. Or perhaps someone you know *knew better* but gradually became more intimate with someone of the opposite sex until it became adultery.

For the sake of our own well-being, as well as for the sake of others, we are called to live by the example that Jesus set for us. We are called to live well. That means that we listen to the voice inside us that tells us right from wrong. We are to listen to and heed the inner call of God's Spirit with a resounding, *Yes, I do know better.* But there's more. Our will kicks in and then moves us into decision-making mode that has *love neighbor as self* as the first filter to separate what we should do from what we should not do.

This process requires us to be intentional, thoughtful, and discerning as we discover how freedom and love fit together. Love, when freely exercised, creates more freedom for others as well as for ourselves. Paul's images of "biting and devouring each other" display how selfishness erodes the goodness of any community (5:15). Our discipleship is not lived out in a vacuum, but truly in connection with others. Indeed, living in ways that indulge the sinful nature erodes our own freedom and eventually destroys community, connection, and fellowship with others.

## The Sinful Nature (5:16–18)

What are we to do with Paul's statement that the desires of the "sinful nature" (NIV) or "flesh" (NRSV, NASB) are "contrary to the Spirit"? After all, when we read Genesis, we find that God looked at *all* creation and said it was "very good" (Genesis 1:31).

Paul was not saying that material things or our human, physical desires are evil in themselves.[1]

Essentially, Paul was saying that we have two choices by which to live life. We can base all of our choices on either the natural world (the flesh) that we see or on the things we cannot see (the Spirit). Paul was calling the

Galatian church to make decisions based on the invisible and intangible way of the Spirit, in opposition to the pull to base their thinking on earthly things.

Too, Paul was not simply creating a list of *don'ts*. That would have put him right back under the law he argued so strongly against.

## Acts of the Sinful Nature (5:19–21)

In naming these acts, Paul was pointing out that we should place all our hope for fulfillment and soul-level satisfaction in the things of the Spirit, not in the things of the flesh. Consider how each of the following actions falls short of the true satisfaction that is desired.

"Sexual immorality, impurity and debauchery"—sexual sins—may leave the flesh temporarily satisfied, but ultimately one's spiritual side is left feeling empty and alone. The companionship of physical connection is unfulfilling outside of a covenant relationship.

"Idolatry and witchcraft" put vague attempts at spirituality ahead of God's place as the singular object of our worship and adoration. The false gods of pleasure, entertainment, and other religions ultimately leave a hole in our being.

"Hatred, discord, jealousy, fits of rage, dissensions, factions, and envy" are all things that build up enmity between us and others. Gossiping about another person may feel good temporarily, as may *blowing your top* in a fit of rage. Perhaps you have had occasion to deal with the after-effects of such behavior. Cleaning up those kinds of messes in relationships can be difficult at best, and often leads to the ultimate destruction of a relationship.

"Selfish ambition" may well be the greatest challenge in our current culture. One of the problems is that it is so easily and readily affirmed, even within the church, especially when it leads to material success.

"Drunkenness" and "orgies" both refer in their own way to loss of control over our selves. Those who engage in such behaviors are often seeking release from stress. They believe that if they just *let go* for a while the stress will go away. Uptight people may well need stress relief, but the way of the Spirit calls for finding such relief in other ways—through such means as prayer, worship, and fellowship with other believers.

Paul added a curious phrase at the end of the list of sinful acts in 5:21—"and the like." That's similar to the legal language that reads, *all of these, but not limited to.* Paul recognized his list was not exhaustive. Other actions beyond those Paul named can signify we are indulging the flesh rather than the Spirit. Paul's addition of this phrase makes the passage timeless in application. The discerning follower of Christ will always be on the lookout for indulgences that distract us from walking with the Spirit.

Paul closed verse 21 with a sobering thought. Those who live in the ways of the flesh will not inherit the kingdom of God. Very real consequences occur in choosing to live a life that gratifies the sinful desires. The statement seems to suggest that anyone who engages in any of the list of sins will simply be kept out of the kingdom. But such a statement would be contrary to Paul's earlier writings about grace and freedom from the law. What Paul was calling for was a careful attentiveness to living life under the guidance of the Spirit, a life that results in the higher righteousness, a higher standard of living.

## Acts of the Spirit (5:22–26)

Because Galatians 5:13–26 is meant to portray responsibility in the context of freedom, Paul concluded with imagery of what that responsibility looks like. The fruit of the Spirit are pieces of evidence that we are following the Spirit in our lives. We see the evidence of the Spirit's presence when

- We see someone living with joy despite adversity in his or her life.
- We see someone choose goodness even though surrounded by evil.
- We see someone keep a commitment when he or she could shirk responsibility.

- We see someone return a rude gesture on the freeway with a kind smile and wave.

All of these examples show specifics of how the Spirit works though believers to make a real, even though small, difference. When we walk by the Spirit, we bear fruit. If, though, we circle back to how Paul began—with the command to love others as self—we can infer that the fruit of the Spirit are not actually *for us* but *for others.* Thus, the fruit of the Spirit are qualities we give away, not things we accumulate or horde for ourselves.

Bearing "the fruit of the Spirit" means we become "other-directed" in the midst of a consumer culture that hordes for self-serving reasons.[2] Consider how this thought speaks to your participation in the life of your church. Do you attend worship or Bible study so you *can get something out of it?* Or, do you look for how you can contribute or add to how your entire church *walks in the Spirit?*

When we bear the fruit of the Spirit into others' lives, we become Christlike, and we also clear out space for others to foster a Christ-like nature. Paul exhorted the Galatians to "keep in step with the Spirit" (Gal. 5:25). Like holding a formation in a marching band or a military march, walking in step with the Spirit is necessary to make the community strong.

## Implications and Actions

Through his Letter to the Galatians, Paul is encouraging *us* to walk by the Spirit. For Christians to walk by the Spirit, we have to weigh out the implications of our freedom in Christ. Do we use our freedom to advance our own agenda? Paul framed it clearly for us. We are to strive hard after loving neighbor as self.

That's a challenge for even the *best* Christians. How do we do it? We begin by accepting the gift of God's grace, understanding that the free gift also includes a call to subscribe to a higher standard of living. Such a standard is not met by satisfying the laws of Moses but by choosing the Spirit over the sinful nature. It is a standard that is met when we imitate Christ. It is a standard that is met when we are other-directed with our love.

This text calls us to self-examination. We do well to look honestly at whether we are willing to share the fruit of the Spirit as a way of walking in the Spirit.

## HOW DO WE HANDLE THE RESPONSIBILITY OF FREEDOM?

God's grace provides us freedom from the law. God's grace also has ethical implications! How are we to handle our freedoms? Suppose, for example, you have enough money to drive any vehicle you want, regardless of purchase cost or operating expense. Is it okay for you to buy a vehicle that is more than you need or is it more loving of others and of creation to purchase only what you need?

## "THE FRUIT OF THE SPIRIT"

1. Review the fruit of the Spirit in Galatians 5:22–23. What is a practical way each one of "the fruit of the Spirit" (5:22–23) can be expressed?

2. Which of "the fruit of the Spirit" most needs to be expressed in the life of *your church* right now?

3. Which of "the fruit of the Spirit" most needs to be expressed in *your life* right now?

## QUESTIONS

1. Where have you seen the Spirit at work recently? How have you been a part of that work?

2. Consider the examples of the fruit of the Spirit listed
   (bulleted items) in the section "Acts of the Spirit
   (5:22–26)." What other examples could you add?

3. How do you discern the difference between actions
   that are indulgent of the sinful nature from actions
   that are a part of your freedom in Christ?

4. We often are better at identifying the acts of a sinful
   nature (Gal. 5:19–21) in others, but what would
   happen in our church if we worked harder to identify
   the fruit of the Spirit at work in others?

5. Why is living by the Spirit (5:16) more effective in guiding right behavior than is keeping rules?

6. What are some reasons "the fruit of the Spirit" (5:22–23) are to be preferred over the "acts of the sinful nature" (5:19–21)?

NOTES ————————————————————————

1. Charles B. Cousar, *Galatians*, Interpretation: A Bible Commentary for Teaching and Preaching (Louisville, Kentucky: John Knox Press, 1982), 137.

2. Phillip D. Kenneson, *Life on the Vine—Cultivating the Fruit of the Spirit in Christian Community* (Downers Grove, Illinois: InterVarsity Press, 1999).

LESSON EIGHT

*Life in a Good Church*

## MAIN IDEA

Positive church life includes offering help even to members who have sinned, humbly examining one's own life, supporting church leaders, never giving up in doing good, and continually focusing on Christ.

## QUESTION TO EXPLORE

What's life like in a truly good church?

## STUDY AIM

To evaluate our church in light of Paul's teachings on how the church is to conduct itself and decide on at least one action I will take to help our church in light of this evaluation

## QUICK READ

Life in a good church involves all kinds of sharing—including sharing burdens, resources, a harvest, and the gospel.

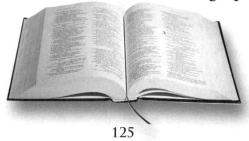

Life in a good church is elusive for some because their church is not living up to the call to be the body of Christ. For others, life in a good church is actually happening. Grounded in realism about the human bent to sin, members of some churches seem to get along with one another well, while other churches are not so peaceful.

So how can a congregation become a *good church*? A major part of the answer is the principle of sharing seen in this passage.

## GALATIANS 6:1–10, 14–16

[1] Brothers, if someone is caught in a sin, you who are spiritual should restore him gently. But watch yourself, or you also may be tempted. [2] Carry each other's burdens, and in this way you will fulfill the law of Christ. [3] If anyone thinks he is something when he is nothing, he deceives himself. [4] Each one should test his own actions. Then he can take pride in himself, without comparing himself to somebody else, [5] for each one should carry his own load.

[6] Anyone who receives instruction in the word must share all good things with his instructor.

[7] Do not be deceived: God cannot be mocked. A man reaps what he sows. [8] The one who sows to please his sinful nature, from that nature will reap destruction; the one who sows to please the Spirit, from the Spirit will reap eternal life. [9] Let us not become weary in doing good, for at the

proper time we will reap a harvest if we do not give up. **10** Therefore, as we have opportunity, let us do good to all people, especially to those who belong to the family of believers.

• • • • • • • • • • • • • • • • • • • •

**14** May I never boast except in the cross of our Lord Jesus Christ, through which the world has been crucified to me, and I to the world. **15** Neither circumcision nor uncircumcision means anything; what counts is a new creation. **16** Peace and mercy to all who follow this rule, even to the Israel of God.

## Share the Burdens (6:1–5)

In Galatians 6:1–5, Paul was giving instruction about the restoration of one who had fallen prey to sin and had been cut off from fellowship. He was also addressing the responsibility to bear one another's burdens as the church shared life together. Pairing these two ideas in one section of text suggests that Paul believed that relationships and restoration were more important than the so-called purity of the institution of church.

Paul urged congregations to restore gently an offending brother or sister into the fellowship of the church, a kind of gentleness that would leave room for the offender to hold on to some degree of dignity. Paul also warned that no matter how the restoration was carried out, care and caution should be exercised in order that others were not drawn into the same plight. Think here of a Christian who began with good intentions, going out after a wayward brother or sister to help the person find a way back to the fellowship of the church, only to be caught in similar circumstances. Paul urged prudence in this regard. Verse 2 may suggest that we should do this work together. We are to "carry each other's burdens, and in this way you will fulfill the law of Christ" (Galatians 6:2).

The law of Christ, summed up by Paul in Galatians 5:14, is the law of love. Carrying one another's burdens is a way by which we can love one another as Christ loves us. At the heart of this issue is that Christ's redeeming love should be allowed to shape the manner in which we show love to others, whether they are in the good graces of the fellowship or cut off from the church by their sin.

The modern church reading this passage could find several implications. One is that relationships always trump institutions in importance. In other words, it's more important for the church to welcome back the penitent sinner regardless of how it makes the church look to others.

Further, this teaching implies that there should always be room at the spiritual table of Christ for anyone, regardless of how messy, confused, or used up they may seem to be. We would do well to read this passage with an awareness of how Jesus welcomed the tax collectors, prostitutes, and lepers when nobody in the religious establishment would make room for them.

Behind this passage, too, is the teaching that all of us are sinners who will from time to time require restoration. How we treat others in such situations may foretell the way in which our heavenly Father will treat us, as in the parable of the unforgiving servant (Matthew 18:21–33).

## Carry Your Load While You Share the Burdens (6:5)

In Galatians 6:5, note what seems to be a contradiction to 6:2. Verse 2 reads, "Carry each other's burdens," and verse 5 reads, "for each one should carry his own load." English translations vary on verse 5, but the Greek would be more properly rendered into English as "each one *will* carry his own load" (future tense; italics for emphasis). Paul might have been referring to an ultimate day where each person will stand independently before God to answer for his or her own actions. This, then, does not relieve us of the command in 6:2 to "carry each other's burdens." Some loads are our responsibilities to carry alone; other heavy burdens can be shared.

To share the burdens of life is one of the sweetest benefits of being a participant in the life of a good church. When life is hard and you and your family are beset by challenges, a good church shares the difficulties with you by providing care, support, prayer, and encouragement through hard times. Sharing the burdens others carry can prove to be one of the most rewarding forms of ministry in which any Christian can engage. To know that you've *been there* for someone in a difficult place in the person's journey is deeply satisfying and fulfilling, not to mention that it honors Jesus by caring for another part of Christ's body. The beauty of this type of fellowship shines brightest when we love one another in the same way Christ loves us.

This type of fellowship was a goal Paul had for his other beloved congregations, in addition to the Galatian church. For example, 1 Corinthians 12 describes the interplay of exercising our own spiritual gifts and sharing in the body of Christ. Specifically, he wrote, "If one part suffers, every part suffers with it; if one part is honored, every part rejoices with it" (1 Corinthians 12:26).

Consider the many ways this happens in your own congregation. How does your church family respond when someone dies? What are the meaningful customs that are enacted to bring care to a bereaved family? Or consider the ways in which a congregation celebrates joyous occasions such as weddings, births, and baptisms. Not only do these rituals of care provide a framework of meaning, they show real care, ministry, and devotion to the work of fellowship. Sharing burdens is a major portion of life in a good church.

## Share the Resources (6:6)

Some might argue this is a favorite passage for a pastor to read as devotional material to the personnel committee of your church just before the annual review and the new budget. It is not inaccurate, though, to use this verse to remind congregants of the need to compensate the church's ministers properly. It is plausible, too, that Paul was using this verse to make a case for the offering he was collecting for the Christians in the Jerusalem church, and, since the teaching apostles were based there, Paul was using this as an opportunity to put in a good word for the offering.

There are many ways congregations can fulfill the obligation to provide compensation or support for ministers. One way is by providing appropriate compensation for the pastors and staff currently employed by your church. Many clergy have invested much time and money in their education, but they will earn far less money than other professions with similar schooling lengths. Local churches honor the calling and ordination of all ministers by striving to pay ministers as well as each church can, rather than the approach of *getting the best bargain* for a minister.

Another way of honoring this obligation is to support theological education. Churches need theologically-trained ministers who are able to lead congregations. Very few people are able to devote time and money to gaining theological training without assistance. The local church contributes to the larger causes of the kingdom of God by supporting the work of partner institutions that prepare people for vocational ministry.

A third way a congregation can respond to this scriptural obligation is to serve as a training field for ministerial candidates. Some churches—small and large—have a special calling to serve as places where fledgling clergy are able to gain practical experience in ministry. Larger churches can budget to provide for internships that give valuable experiences for ministers in training.

The church of the future will always need ministers. Your church can plant good seeds that will produce a good harvest for future congregations. You could be supporting the training for a minister who will baptize your great-grandchildren!

## Share the Harvest (6:7–10)

Life in a good church means that the congregation will look for opportunities to sow good seeds that lead to reaping "eternal life" (Gal. 6:8). Persistence in sowing is the crux of the message here. Paul wrote in verse 9, "Let us not become weary." Later in the same verse he wrote about not giving up. Paul implored the Galatian Christians not to give up on "doing good" just because there were no short-term results. He suggested by way of the sowing/reaping metaphor that the "harvest" would come in due time.

Waiting to share the harvest as a congregation is counter-cultural in a society that emphasizes the quick fix, high-speed efficiency, and instant results. Paul suggested that in God's economy there is little room for those who would pursue immediate gratification. Paul emphasized the need for "doing good" for the long haul.

## Share the Gospel (6:14–16)

Paul closed the letter with a postscript aimed directly at those in the Galatian church who were boasting about converting people to be circumcised, thus emphasizing the need to keep the traditions of Judaism in order to become a Christian. Paul countered their boasting by saying that he would only "boast in the cross of our Lord Jesus Christ" (6:14).

Paul's boasting in the cross becomes a pattern for us. In adversity, Paul emphasized the cross of Christ. In joyous times, Paul emphasized the cross of Christ. In season or out of season, Paul's boasting made the story of the cross known. Paul's boasting in the cross was one of the ways in which he was able to share the gospel of Jesus. Life in a good church includes sharing the gospel in multiple ways.

For Paul, the story of what Christ had done for him was the defining and pivotal moment of his life. His conversion to Christ on the Damascus road left him in a place where he simply could not keep quiet. Everywhere Paul went, he boasted of Christ crucified and Christ resurrected, and how he had been changed forever by an encounter with the resurrected Christ. Paul went from being a persecutor of Christians and ardent keeper of the law to the complete opposite position of being a zealous Christian and an eloquent proponent of freedom in Christ by way of grace through faith.

Paul's boasting in the cross was meant to share the gospel, and that gospel included a freedom from the law. More specific to the Galatians, that meant a freedom from circumcision, and in fact a freedom from even arguing the point of circumcision.

Truly, to experience life in a good church means moving away from legalism and toward a caring evangelism. Sharing the gospel is part of life in a good church, the gospel that brings peace and mercy to all who would accept it.

## Implications and Actions

Life in a good church involves lots of flexibility, faithfulness, and love. There's an old saying, "The grass is greener on the other side of the fence." That saying is disproved by Paul's advice to the Galatians and could perhaps be reworded to read, *The grass is greener where you water it.*

While it may be tempting for us to move to a new church when fellowship is disrupted, the early Christians, including these at Galatia, had no such luxury. Paul's directives in this passage may be calling us to see the importance of staying put, tending to our relationships, and bearing with one another in grace and patience. Of course, doing this is easier said than done sometimes. But for those who have experienced life in a good church, the labor is well worth the investment. Be encouraged to hang in there with your church in good and hard times!

## REAPING AND SOWING

When I was growing up on a farm in southeastern North Carolina, my favorite time of the summer came when we harvested the crop and took it to the warehouse for sale. I could see the results of our work and appreciate all those hot, sweaty days of labor I'd invested alongside others.

That September day would not have been possible unless someone started with seeds in March and then in April transplanted thousands of plants by hand to the field where they grew under the farmer's watchful eye. Fertilizer, sunshine, water, good soil, and a lot of hard work combined to make the crop.

We got what we sowed. Everything that we put in added to the yield we reaped. If one step had been skipped the crop might have survived, but it would have been less fruitful. If several steps were omitted, the crop likely would have been a disaster.

The same is true in our spiritual lives. What we invest will affect the yield. If we sow seeds to please our sinful nature, destruction will be our fruit. If we sow to please the Spirit, we reap eternal life. What kinds of seed are you sowing?

## LIFE IN A GOOD CHURCH INVOLVES SHARING

- *Sharing the burdens.* The sweetest part of fellowship is caring for one another in times of joy and sorrow.

- *Carry your load while you share the burdens.* All of the responsibilities of the church are meant to be shared by everyone, not just by a few.

- *Sharing the resources.* Congregations have the responsibility to provide financial security for its pastor and staff.

- *Sharing the harvest.* Churches are called to sow and reap, with an eye on the long-term harvest of eternity.

- *Sharing the gospel.* Paul boasted in the cross of Christ as a way of sharing the gospel. Churches today should do the same!

## EXPRESSING CARE

When my mother died, the church family at Pleasant Plains Baptist Church fed our family. The casseroles, with their accompanying hugs and tears, covered the kitchen counter to the point you couldn't even see the formica. The pastor led a worship gathering in which it seemed the congregation was lifting me up into God's lap for solace and tenderness. What does your congregation do to express care for folk in grief? When have you been cared for in a similar way?

## HOW DOES SIN AFFECT YOUR CHURCH?

A deacon from a small-town Baptist church was caught in an illegal embezzlement scheme. Much of the town gossiped, wondering—among other things—whether the church would have him resign as a deacon. The deacon voluntarily resigned because he understood that his actions reflected badly on the deacons and the whole church. He then confessed his sin to the congregation and asked their forgiveness.

What does this passage of Scripture and this example of the deacon suggest about dealing with someone in the church who "is caught in a sin" (Gal. 6:1)?

## QUESTIONS

1. Have you ever been in a church where someone was "disciplined" or cut off from fellowship because of sin? Was the person welcomed back eventually? What does Paul mean by "restore him gently" (Gal. 6:1)?

2. Why do you think Paul warned that caution should be taken "or you also may be tempted" (6:2) when restoring someone?

3. How should a church determine compensation for a minister?

4. How have you experienced "life in a good church"?

5. What other things should a good church share besides those things listed in the lesson comments?

6. In what did Paul boast? Why was that the source of Paul's boasting?

7. The lesson suggests that members of a good church will share burdens, share the resources, share the harvest, and share the gospel. What else would you add? Is there anything you'd take away?

# Introducing

# 1 AND 2 THESSALONIANS:
# Guidance for Healthy Church Life

## Letters to a Young Church

The two letters to the Christians at Thessalonica reveal the great concern of Paul the missionary for the young church he and the missionary leadership team had established there. Paul and his fellow missionaries had established the church on Paul's second missionary journey, toward the midpoint of the first century A.D. (see Acts 17:1–9). According to Acts, the missionary leadership team had come to Thessalonica after establishing the church at Philippi. Thessalonica was in the Roman province of Macedonia, the same province as Philippi.

The account in Acts of the establishment of the church in Thessalonica shows the intense pressure the young church must have been under when Paul later wrote them.

They were the first Christians in their community, and they faced great opposition. Out of continued missionary concern for the Thessalonian Christians and a desire to provide them further instructions on some questions they had, Paul wrote back to them. The result is our two New Testament letters, 1 and 2 Thessalonians.

## 1 and 2 Thessalonians in the New Testament

First Thessalonians is the oldest letter of Paul, having been written about 49–50 A.D. Mark, the first of the four Gospels, likely was not written until the mid–60s. The Book of James may be the oldest New Testament book, but it is also possible that 1 Thessalonians itself is the very earliest New Testament book to have been written.

## Studying 1 and 2 Thessalonians

First and Second Thessalonians resemble each other in structure, and each contains some elements that remind us of the other. In each letter, Paul began by giving thanks for the church at Thessalonica. In the first lesson in 1 Thessalonians, which is lesson nine in this study, we will seek to discover qualities we can apply to our own churches (1 Thessalonians 1; 2:13–14, 19–20; 3:6–9; 2 Thessalonians 1:1–4).

Especially in 1 Thessalonians, Paul described the way in which he and the missionary team sought to give leadership to the Thessalonians. The second lesson on 1 and 2 Thessalonians thus looks at the qualities of leadership that Paul commended and the missionary team demonstrated (1 Thess. 2:1–12; 5:12–13). This lesson will call us to consider the kind of leadership we ourselves value. Sooner or later every church will need to consider this theme, for every church will seek a pastor or staff member or will select lay leaders. Each church thus needs to consider what kind of leaders it will seek.

The third lesson on 1 and 2 Thessalonians focuses on Paul's instructions about living so as to please God and win the respect of others (1 Thess. 4:1–12; 5:14–24). This lesson will challenge us to measure our lives by each of these important areas and to determine ways we will live so as to please God and win the respect of other people, especially people outside the church. This lesson is especially important in light of the negative view many people outside the church have of Christians.

The fourth lesson in the study of 1 and 2 Thessalonians treats a theme that appears in both letters—the Christian hope and the return of Christ (1 Thess. 4:13—5:11; 2 Thess. 1:5—2:12). Our study will emphasize the treatment of this theme in 1 Thessalonians 4:13—5:11. This passage, particularly 1 Thessalonians 4:13–18, has long been the source of great help to Christians who have lost loved ones. As we study the Christian hope in this lesson, the message for the Thessalonian Christians and for us is to "encourage one another with these words" (1 Thess. 4:18), rather than to fear or ignore them.[1] Studying this passage can enable us to understand what the hope Christ offers means for our lives now and as we consider eternity for ourselves and others.

The final lesson in the study focuses on the instructions Paul offered the young church about how to be a thriving church in a tough situation (2 Thess. 3). These instructions can provide guidance to a church in almost any situation.

### 1 & 2 THESSALONIANS: GUIDANCE FOR HEALTHY CHURCH LIFE

| | | |
|---|---|---|
| Lesson 9 | Thank God for Such a Church! | 1 Thessalonians 1 |
| Lesson 10 | The Leadership God Wants | 1 Thessalonians 2:1–12 |
| Lesson 11 | Live to Please God and Win Others' Respect | 1 Thessalonians 4:1–12; 5:14–24 |
| Lesson 12 | Hope for Time and Eternity | 1 Thessalonians 4:13—5:11 |
| Lesson 13 | Being a Thriving Church in a Tough Situation | 2 Thessalonians 3:1–16 |

Additional Resources for Studying 1 and 2 Thessalonians:[2]

F.F. Bruce. *1 & 2 Thessalonians*. Word Biblical Commentary. Volume 45. Waco, Texas: Word Books, Inc., 1982.

Gary W. Demarest. *1, 2 Thessalonians; 1, 2 Timothy; and Titus*. The Comunicator's Commentary. Volume 9. Waco, TX: Word Books, Inc., 1984.

Beverly Roberts Gaventa. *First and Second Thessalonians.* Interpretation: A Bible Commentary for Teaching and Preaching. Louisville: John Knox Press, 1998.

Herschel H. Hobbs. "1—2 Thessalonians." *The Broadman Bible Commentary.* Volume 11. Nashville, Tennessee: Broadman Press, 1971.

Craig S. Keener. *IVP Bible Background Commentary: New Testament.* Downers Grove, Illinois: InterVarsity Press, 1993.

Leon Morris. *The First and Second Epistles to the Thessalonians.* The New International Commentary on the New Testament. Grand Rapids, Michigan: Eerdmans, 1959, 1982.

A.T. Robertson. *Word Pictures in the New Testament.* Volume IV, The Epistles of Paul. Nashville, Tennessee: Broadman Press, 1931.

Abraham Smith. "The First Letter to the Thessalonians" and "The Second Letter to the Thessalonians." *The New Interpreter's Bible.* Volume XI. Nashville: Abingdon Press, 2000.

# NOTES

1. Unless otherwise indicated, all Scripture quotations in "Introducing 1 and 2 Thessalonians: Guidance for Healthy Church Life" and lessons 9–13 are from the New International Version.

2. Listing a book does not imply full agreement by the writers or BAPTISTWAY PRESS® with all of its comments.

**FOCAL TEXT**

1 Thessalonians 1

**BACKGROUND**

1 Thessalonians 1; 2:13–14;
3:6–9; 2 Thessalonians
1:1–4; 2:13

LESSON NINE

# *Thank God for Such a Church!*

## MAIN IDEA

Thank God for a church that is an example to others in faith, hope, and love.

## QUESTION TO EXPLORE

For what about your church do you thank God?

## STUDY AIM

To identify qualities of my church for which I thank God and express thanks to God as I identify positive qualities in it

## QUICK READ

Thessalonica was a model church—a good church but not a perfect church. Examining the good qualities of this church can lead you to appreciate and commit yourself more deeply to the present and potential impact that your church can have.

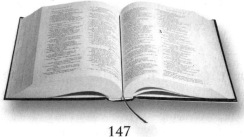

The instruction "say *thank you*" is repeated often to young children. Parents recognize the importance of such training, knowing that their children are better off when they learn to respond positively to acts of kindness and helpfulness. Children may do this well with outsiders while not always being too happy to respond in the same way to a brother or sister. Regardless, underlying thanksgiving is the growing awareness that we are not independent creatures flying solo through the universe, but we are interdependent people. Ultimately, we need to learn to recognize the greatest truth about thanksgiving—that God has abundantly blessed us. We depend on God, and so we should willingly show our gratitude.

Thessalonica was a major city in the first century, active in trade and commerce and enabled by the Romans to be a free city. Alexander the Great had lived in Macedonia, and the area was greatly influenced by Athenian and Roman culture and religion. Jews also populated the city. Paul and his missionary companions went to Thessalonica after Paul had a vision of a man from Macedonia begging him to "come over to Macedonia and help us" (Acts 16:9). Paul and Silas made several stops before arriving in Thessalonica (Acts 17). They ministered there for about two weeks before irate Jews and others trumped up false charges against them and went in search of them. When the mob could not find Paul and Silas at Jason's house, they dragged Jason, a convert in Thessalonica, before city officials. Although the city was in an uproar, they allowed Jason to post bond and let him go.

Paul and Silas left Thessalonica in the night and went on to Berea. Eventually Paul made his way to Athens, then Corinth, where Timothy brought him a report about the church in Thessalonica. Paul responded to this news with a letter of encouragement to the Thessalonians.

# 1 THESSALONIANS 1

**1** Paul, Silas and Timothy,

To the church of the Thessalonians in God the Father and the Lord Jesus Christ:

Grace and peace to you.

**2** We always thank God for all of you, mentioning you in our prayers. **3** We continually remember before our God and Father your work produced by faith, your labor prompted by love, and your endurance inspired by hope in our Lord Jesus Christ.

**4** For we know, brothers loved by God, that he has chosen you, **5** because our gospel came to you not simply with words, but also with power, with the Holy Spirit and with deep conviction. You know how we lived among you for your sake. **6** You became imitators of us and of the Lord; in spite of severe suffering, you welcomed the message with the joy given by the Holy Spirit. **7** And so you became a model to all the believers in Macedonia and Achaia. **8** The

Lord's message rang out from you not only in Macedonia and Achaia—your faith in God has become known everywhere. Therefore we do not need to say anything about it, **9** for they themselves report what kind of reception you gave us. They tell how you turned to God from idols to serve the living and true God, **10** and to wait for his Son from heaven, whom he raised from the dead—Jesus, who rescues us from the coming wrath.

## Thanksgiving (1:1–2)

Thanksgiving is always in season; it's not just something we celebrate in November. As blessed people, we have many reasons for thanksgiving. Like Paul, one of these reasons occurs when we hear good reports about how dear friends are doing. "We always thank God for all of you" (1 Thessalonians 1:2) was not flattery. Paul's sincere thanksgiving for the Thessalonians is repeated in 2:13 and 3:9, as well as in the follow-up letter of 2 Thessalonians (1:3 and 2:13). Paul could hardly think of the Thessalonian people without breaking out in thanksgiving.

Paul did not live among the Thessalonians long, but they were still dear to him. Paul was thankful for their faithfulness to God in difficult circumstances, as well as their helpfulness to him.

We live in a *what have you done for me lately?* kind of world. We sometimes forget the grace of God and the blessings that come our way because of him. Some may fall into the common trap and think like the people of the Old Testament did, that "my power and the strength of my hands have produced this wealth for me" (Deuteronomy 8:17). We can become smug and forget the blessings that come with citizenship, in the kingdom of God as well as in our country. We may forget our dependence on God and our interdependence on one another. We often have a short memory about the need for gratitude, but that does not have to be the case. With purposeful thankful living and regular thanksgiving, you can live a lifestyle that honors God and is a blessing to others.

## Qualities of a Model Church (1:3–8)

I think about reading books in two different ways. One method is what I call *point of a pencil* reading. With this method, I read, highlight, and take notes, attempting to recall and understand what I have just read. I often used this method in school and in professional work. Now, I spend more time in *recreational reading*—reading simply for the joy of the book. Chapter one of 1 Thessalonians is a *point of a pencil* read. You could circle key words as you read, and you would end up with a long list of important words. You could make a list of significant teachings, and you would almost duplicate the Scripture itself. Every sentence in this chapter reveals important truth and is appropriate for developing a profile of a healthy church.

The church at Thessalonica was a model church, characterized by faith, hope, and love (1 Thess. 1:3). They were active, and their work was produced by faith. Faith can be described in many ways, but it always involves (1) receiving from God what God has to offer and (2) yielding to God what God demands. A model church is characterized by both faith and work, and it is inspired and empowered by love. God is the source of that love, but the delivery system for God's love includes people who are willing to allow God's perspective and presence to be channeled through their lives. The model church also stays at the task, as is suggested by the word "endurance." Its members do not quit before the game is over. They endure because they have an enduring hope in Christ Jesus.

Further, model churches know who they are and why they exist. God "has chosen you" (1 Thess. 1:4) is a reminder that God takes the initiative in calling the church into being. (The "you" is plural.) He loves us and chooses for us to be in his family. This does not imply that God chooses some and ignores others, for it is not God's will that anyone should perish (2 Peter 3:9). We have not discovered God on our own, but God has revealed himself to us and has chosen us to be part of his family. As such, we are brothers and sisters, "loved by God" (1 Thess. 1:4). That's our identity. As John later wrote, "How great is the love the Father has lavished on us, that we should be called children of God! And that is what we are" (1 John 3:1). Model churches understand their identity as God's children.

But a model church is more than just a collection of brothers and sisters in Christ. Here, the power of God's Spirit is allowed to move freely in the life of the church. First Thessalonians 1:5 confirms what Acts 2 reveals: the church that God created is empowered by God's Spirit. God has made himself available to us in a unique way, so that any congregation can be greater than the sum of its individual, human parts. Thessalonica did not become a model congregation on its own, and neither did it continue to do great things apart from God. This power source is also reflected by words of the prophet Zechariah, "'not by might nor by power, but by my Spirit,' says the LORD Almighty" (Zech. 4:6).

Although empowered by God, a model church also needs good examples to follow (1 Thess. 1:6). Paul was not being arrogant when he wrote that the Thessalonians used him as an example. They were young Christians, and they needed a good example. Paul, Silas, and Timothy filled that need. Obviously, within the church at Thessalonica, other people provided good examples as well. These new leaders continued the cycle of caring for people, developing believers, and reaching out to those who were not followers of Jesus. The Thessalonians had a genuine conversion—they turned from idolatry and toward Jesus. In the process, they served God with patience and endurance. They were standing "firm in the Lord" (1 Thess. 3:8).

A model church handles rejection and persecution positively. The Thessalonians experienced "severe suffering" (1:6). Not everyone liked them (2:13–14), but Paul liked the way they handled adversity (2 Thess. 1:4). The church at Thessalonica experienced the same kind of rejection and oppression that Christians had suffered in other first-century places. Considering what happened to Jesus, should anyone be surprised?

Although Jesus warned his followers about persecution and suffering, his forewarning does not eliminate all the pain and consequences of unjust treatment. When rejection occurs, we should heed what Jesus told his followers: "shake the dust off your feet" and move on (Matthew 10:14). Jesus also taught in the Beatitudes that persecuted followers of his would one day be blessed (Matt. 5:11–12) and rewarded. Fortunately, most of us have never experienced that kind of persecution, but it exists in many places in our world today. Even if we have not experienced persecution for being a follower of Jesus, the way we handle other issues of suffering and misfortune may still allow us to be a positive, shining example to others.

A model church continues to grow in its relationship with God and with one another. Paul knew the Thessalonians were exemplary people. Even so, when further word came back to him about their lives while he was in Corinth, he commended them for faith that was growing and love for each other that was increasing (2 Thess. 1:3). He gave thanksgiving to God for the continued spiritual growth in their lives.

A man told me, "I believe the same things now that I believed at twelve years of age. I have not changed a bit." At that time, I did not know him well enough to evaluate his comment too deeply, but I later thought, "I may have had some commendable beliefs and virtues at age twelve, but I pray that I'm not the same as I was then. I pray that he is mistaken about himself also." God saved us, but God continues to shape and mold us for a lifetime. The Thessalonians were not the same folks that Paul knew earlier. They had grown. That's the way it should be. The Bible says that Jesus "grew in wisdom and stature, and in favor with God and men" (Luke 2:52). Would God expect anything different from us?

## A Servant People (1:9–10)

"To serve the living and true God" (1 Thess. 1:9) is an awesome privilege and responsibility. Think about it—the God of this universe has enough confidence in us that we are chosen to represent him. He chooses us to serve him. Lordship is reserved for God; servanthood is designed for us. We are not in the world to rule over people or to change another person's cultural heritage. We are in the world to serve God, sharing the presence and message of Christ to others as we wait for Christ's return (1:10). When we do that, we walk in the lineage of people like the Thessalonians.

As we shall see in further study, the Thessalonian church was not perfect. They had issues of faith and practice that needed attention. However, they were effectively making an impact where they lived, and that impact had ripple effects that touched many other people and places. They were a model example, but they were not perfect. Luckily, God does not depend on perfect people to make a difference. Certainly, the Thessalonians could have done better (as can we all), and we will study in the next lesson how Paul encouraged them to do so.

Early in my seminary experience, I read some graffiti written on a chalkboard: "He who preaches on that which is perfect in his own life has no text on which to preach." That word from an unusual source stuck with me. I preached and now write, not because I have everything worked out perfectly, but because I am continually growing. None of us have it all worked out. God's grace takes us where we are and continues to shape us into what God wants us to be. The quest to find a perfect church is futile, but a servant body who wants to make a difference for our Lord is still a model to others. It is our time to serve, and qualities such as those Paul identified in Thessalonica are still appropriate for us to mirror today.

## Taking It Personally

We often read materials and comprehend them. We may even say, "That was good." But sometimes after our studies, we walk away without making any change or personal application to our lives. Even a writer can do that. It's easy for me to be impressed with the Thessalonians. Too, I admire Paul for commending them for their strengths. We can all gather information and understanding from this text. But then what do we do with it? Could we agree on the following list?

- Pray that our church will be a *model* church, embodying the qualities that the Thessalonians displayed.
- Be more thankful and affirming of the good we see in others and in our church.
- Identify specific people, outside the normal range of our contacts, and seek to be an encourager to them.
- Examine time commitments to see whether they are worthy of a member of a servant church.
- Ask God to guide us in continued spiritual growth. The God who inspired the Bible also inspires us to act and to change.

## Grace and Peace

*Grace* and *peace* were typical Greek and Hebrew greetings in the first century. Even though these words may have been common, they gave substance to a greeting, far more than *hello* or *hi.* The author's prayer was that grace and peace would be imparted to his readers.

An old definition of grace is *God's unmerited favor or love.* Grace is not something we earn or deserve, but it is bound up in the way God relates to us. God does not deal with us according to our merits or according to a law, but according to love. Why? Just because that's the way God is. Aren't you glad?

Peace is not just the absence of a storm, as valuable as that is. *Peace* has an impact on the inner core of our being. Paul's wish was that every person would be reconciled to God and thus live in peace. Likewise, we are to be at peace with others and with ourselves.

*Grace* and *peace*—the order is not coincidental. Without God's grace there is no peace. Using these two great words of the Christian faith, Paul greeted the Thessalonians with a blessing and a prayer. "Grace and peace to you" (1Thess. 1:1).

## Vision 2015

You are a member of Vision 2015, a new committee whose goal is to propose what your church will be like by 2015.

Based on qualities in the Thessalonian church, what would you propose to the committee? Be specific about actions inspired by faith, love, and hope. What would enhance your church's ability to be a model congregation? What would detract? Consider what you think the Holy Spirit would lead you to do.

## QUESTIONS

1. For what are you thankful in your church? How does that compare with your church's reputation in the community?

2. Who has been a good example of the Christian faith to you? If they are still living, have you called or written them to thank them for their influence?

3. If you wrote a prayer of affirmation and blessing for your pastor and other church leaders, what would you say?

4. What are you doing that demonstrates that you serve "the living and true God" (1 Thess. 1:9)?

LESSON TEN

# The Leadership God Wants

## MAIN IDEA

The leaders God wants serve God and the church with integrity, gentleness, loving concern, hard work, and persistent faithfulness.

## QUESTION TO EXPLORE

What qualities should a church look for in its leaders?

## STUDY AIM

To identify qualities of church leaders who are to be affirmed and followed

## QUICK READ

Paul demonstrated integrity, gentleness, loving concern, hard work, and persistent faithfulness in his ministry to the Thessalonians. His example has good implications for church leaders who are vital to a church's health.

*The Macedonian News* has found Paul. He is in Corinth. Readers in Macedonia will remember his controversial career here. Prior to his arrival, he had a prison record in Philippi. Somehow he escaped after an earthquake. He stayed only two weeks in Thessalonica, caused quite a ruckus, and would have been thrown into prison if he had been found. A local business leader, Jason, was arrested instead. Soon afterward, Paul and his associates left town. We contacted a few of his friends who still speak highly of him, although it appears his efforts in promoting the new sect of Christianity are a failure.

The modern world might write the story of Paul in that fashion. We are often quick to write *failure* over ventures of faith as well as over people. A new and different effort is tried to reach people, and no one seems to be reached. A new order of worship is tried, and complaints abound. A notorious person is converted and baptized. Then the person slips back into old patterns, and tongues wag, saying, *I knew it. He wasn't for real.*

Paul's Jewish and/or Gentile critics were speaking badly about him, even calling him a failure. Paul dealt forthrightly with the criticism, saying that his readers in Thessalonica knew that his ministry among them was not a failure (1 Thessalonians 2:1). He acknowledged his ministry in Philippi, which included suffering and insults. You can read the story of Paul's ministry in Philippi in Acts 16 and his work in Thessalonica in Acts 17:1–9. Check them out.

As Paul recalled his story in his letter to the Thessalonians, we discover good insights into what kind of leader he was. As you read the Scripture in this lesson, keep in mind that no matter where you are, someone will provide leadership in every church. It's up to church members to make sure these leaders have qualities that will enhance the ministry and health of the church. Obviously, these few verses will not touch on every leadership quality, but the following attributes will go a long way in building up the church.

## 1 THESSALONIANS 2:1–12

[1] You know, brothers, that our visit to you was not a failure. [2] We had previously suffered and been insulted in Philippi, as you know, but with the help of our God we dared to tell you his gospel in spite of strong opposition. [3] For the appeal we make does not spring from error or impure motives, nor are we trying to trick you. [4] On the contrary, we speak as men approved by God to be entrusted with the gospel. We are not trying to please men but God, who tests our hearts. [5] You know we never used flattery, nor did we put on a mask to cover up greed—God is our witness. [6] We were not looking for praise from men, not from you or anyone else.

As apostles of Christ we could have been a burden to you, **7** but we were gentle among you, like a mother caring for her little children. **8** We loved you so much that we were delighted to share with you not only the gospel of God but our lives as well, because you had become so dear to us. **9** Surely you remember, brothers, our toil and hardship; we worked night and day in order not to be a burden to anyone while we preached the gospel of God to you.

**10** You are witnesses, and so is God, of how holy, righteous and blameless we were among you who believed. **11** For you know that we dealt with each of you as a father deals with his own children, **12** encouraging, comforting and urging you to live lives worthy of God, who calls you into his kingdom and glory.

## Integrity (2:2–6)

Paul was zealous in his persecution of Christians before his Damascus Road experience (Acts 9). After he became a Christian, he did not lose his zeal. He became an avid follower of Jesus. He ministered tirelessly and fearlessly among all groups of people. He did not do so in his own strength, for he depended on the "help of our God" (1 Thess. 2:2) to present the gospel to the Thessalonians.

Paul was open; he had no sinister, hidden agendas. He did not play games or politics with people. He was not in the people-pleasing business. His aim was to be "approved by God" (2:4). That was his agenda. He did not embrace error or practice trickery. He did not flatter to impress or use his special position for greedy gain. He bluntly reminded the Thessalonians, "We were not looking for praise from men, not from you or anyone else" (2:6).

Integrity has many synonyms: *honesty, truthfulness, reliability,* and *uprightness*. Its root meaning indicates something that is *well put together, an integer, a whole, not a fraction*. However we define it, most folks appreciate integrity, although we may be a little suspicious of people who promote their own integrity. However, we do not need to be suspicious of Paul's words. He truly had *been there, done that*. The Thessalonians knew of Paul's faithful life among them, even though some may have wavered in recognizing his leadership. The early church depended on apostolic authority. When false teachers passed through, it was good to have evidence of someone like Paul to whom to compare them. He did not seek the approval of the people, but he told it like it needed to be told. Now he was writing it again. His aim was not to please others but to please God. He did not compromise the message or his integrity in order to win friends.

Speaking of integrity, we need to be careful when we choose the role of constant critic. Those who criticized Paul probably thought they were right, even as Paul thought he was right in his pre-Christian days. They may have thought they had the truth, the whole truth, and nothing but the truth. However, the critics of Paul were wrong. Lies, half-truths, slander, misinformation, and disinformation—you name it—sometimes these are said, claiming to be *in the name of Jesus*. If criticism is due, make sure it is given with humility as well as integrity.

## Gentleness (2:6–7)

Some find it unusual that Paul considered himself "gentle." He wrote so plainly and sometimes bluntly that we might think it is contradictory to be confrontational while also being gentle. Paul used the metaphor of a mother caring for her children as an illustration of how he and his coworkers acted among the Thessalonians (2:7). Later, in verse 11, he also referred to a father's role in child development. Parents who love their children deeply also have to provide boundaries and discipline that may not result in immediate gratification from the child's point of view. These parents, however, are entrusted with guiding children into maturity, and that cannot be done without discipline and occasional confrontation. Perhaps the phrase *tough love* helps us to understand the ability to both love and admonish others whom we care about. "Lives worthy of God" (2:12) have clear boundaries and willingly accept spiritual discipline.

"Gentleness" is a fruit of the Spirit (Galatians 5:23). Fruit develops on trees, and when the Spirit of God fills the tree of a person's life, gentleness is one of the fruits that grows. Gentleness is not restricted to one gender and neither is it a sign of weakness. Gentle people are also people of integrity. They love others enough to confront them as well as to console them. Interestingly, when a church member fell into sin in Galatia, Paul wrote, "you who are spiritual should restore him gently" (Galatians 6:1). Integrity is practiced with gentleness and loving concern.

## Loving Concern (2:8)

Paul did not have any inhibitions in saying, *I love you.* He went to Thessalonica as a stranger, stayed only two weeks, but became a lifelong lover of the people there. He told them so. He commented that they had become "so dear" to him, Silas, and Timothy (1 Thess. 2:8). Never underestimate the value of telling someone you love him or her.

I was visiting a big man whose life was ebbing away due to cancer. He was outgoing and cheerful, but very sick. Holding his hand, I leaned over him. We prayed together. As soon as I said "amen," he put his arm around my neck and pulled me close. He kissed me on the cheek and said, "I love you." I kissed him and told him I loved him. He was a gentle man, filled with love. This was not a death-bed change; it was a way of life for him.

Loving concern is expected and given by most pastors. The word *pastor* is rooted in the word for *shepherd*.

Although the pastor is not the ultimate shepherd, the pastor is an under-shepherd on behalf of the Lord (see 1 Peter 5:1–4). The loving concern the pastor demonstrates comes from the Lord, but demonstrating loving concern must not be limited to pastors or church staff. Every church leader needs to have a loving, pastoral heart for others.

## Hard Work (2:9)

Some think work is a curse that comes from God's judgment in the Garden of Eden. When you read the Genesis account, however, you will see that work was part of God's plan from the beginning. Before sin even entered the story, "the LORD God took the man and put him in the Garden of Eden to work it and take care of it" (Genesis 2:15). When sin entered, all of life was affected, including the work we do.

The Bible portrays the importance of workers throughout. God the Creator was a worker. Jesus was a worker. Paul was a worker. There is dignity and necessity about work. Some Thessalonians had problems with work; they were idle (1 Thess. 5:14), but they did not learn that from Paul's example or teaching.

Paul worked hard in his short time at Thessalonica. He worked with leather and was known as a tent maker. He worked hard, as he said, "night and day" (2:9). We might call such a person *a bi-vocational preacher*. But, in a sense,

Paul was not bi-vocational. Rather he was single-minded in his devotion to Christ and his desire to preach the gospel. Paul's vocation was to serve Christ. He also did not want to burden the new converts to Christ by imposing on their limited means or circumstances. So he earned money to support himself. Paul did not say that everyone had to be a tent maker or be bi-vocational. That was not his point.[1] The point was that just as he worked hard, we should do the same in the world and in our churches.

## Persistent Faithfulness (2:10–12)

Paul wrote, "I have fought the good fight, I have finished the race, I have kept the faith (2 Timothy 4:7). He penned these words at the end of his life to Timothy, his partner in ministering to the Thessalonians. Earlier, at Thessalonica, Paul had demonstrated the qualities he wrote about in 2 Timothy. From first to last in his ministry, he was persistently faithful. Paul did not quit, he pressed on in faithful living.

Years ago I heard Dr. Baker James Cauthen speak to a group of senior adults. He had retired after many years as executive secretary of the Foreign Mission Board of the Southern Baptist Convention. Whenever I heard him preach, I was always moved. He stirred the souls of many people. At the senior adult gathering, he said, "Don't quit living until you die." As we age, we have different energies and activities; however, faithfulness is appropriate for any stage in life.

Notice how Paul viewed his lifestyle while with the Thessalonians. He said he was "holy, righteous and blameless" (2:10). He also said his aim in ministering to them was to be "encouraging, comforting and urging you to live lives worthy of God" (1 Thess. 2:12). Paul was not telling his story to glorify himself, but he was using his life as an illustration of what God can enable a person to be and do. Lest we think Paul was too egotistical, he also referred to himself as the worst of sinners (1 Timothy 1:15). God uses persistently faithful people, in spite of our imperfections.

## Responding to Leadership (5:12–13)

In an ideal world, leaders would possess all kinds of wonderful qualities. Each would be a perfect *10*, and all the church members would be virtuous, faithful, and united in working together with their leaders. Unfortunately, that church has not and does not exist. All leaders are at varying points of maturity and giftedness, and most churches have a similar character.

An imperfect world is all we have. That's what we deal with in a free world, tainted to the core by sin but still guided by God. In our imperfect world, even if leaders are not perfect, what response should the church give to them? Again, the whole story is not told in two verses, but we have sound guidance in a few words.

Churches should follow their leaders and respect them (1 Thess. 5:12). Church members should be promoters of peace within the congregation (5:13). Whatever the leadership role, leaders need support. How many church conflicts could be eliminated if we fervently prayed for our leaders? How many steps of faith could be implemented if we were at peace with one another? How many God-sized assignments could be completed if we held church leaders in high regard, not just because of who they are but also especially for the work they do?

Certainly, we could *what if?* these verses; for example, *What if our leader is not very praiseworthy?* We all know stories about leaders who may be dictatorial, arrogant, or immoral. Set that aside for a moment. The disposition of our soul should be to follow and respect leaders in the church. Select leaders who have the right qualities, and then support them. That predisposition can make our churches into models for others to follow.

## Taking It Personally

Church leaders change. That means that the type of leadership within our churches can change. Sometimes leaders move away, step back to let others lead, or go to be with the Lord. If you stay in a church long enough, at some point you will probably need to find a new pastor. Churches may need staff members or lay leaders for various programs. In most churches, replenishing leadership is a continual challenge.

Since no church is perfect, no leader is perfect, and no member is perfect, what should we do? We can throw up our hands and resign ourselves to futility. Or we could take a biblical and realistic view of the matter. We can do the right thing by identifying good qualities in leaders and then supporting them in their positions. Paul wrote, "with the help of our God we dared to tell you his gospel in spite of strong opposition" (2:2). Underline "with the help of our God." With God at work in your life and in the lives of our church leaders, we will see better days. Our job is to be faithful to God and live in the center of God's will. When that happens, God fulfills his promise of working things out for our good (Romans 8:28).

## BAPTIST SCHOOLS

Baptist colleges and universities exist across our country. As you consider the need for church leaders with good qualities, do not neglect to support our Baptist colleges, universities, and seminaries with your prayer, financial support, and personal involvement. These educational institutions play an important role in the preparation for vocational ministry. Remember, too, that Baptist colleges and universities have an important role in preparing laypeople to make a difference in the world. Educated laypeople who are faithful to our Lord and involved in our world can be the biblical light and salt that Jesus mentioned (Matthew 5:13–16). They are vital to our Lord's mission in the local church and around the world.

## LEADERSHIP

Every person is a leader of some person or group in some way. Consider your leadership, however small or large you think your leadership role may be. Using the leadership qualities in today's Scripture, how would your friends and fellow class members rate your integrity, gentleness, loving concern, hard work, and persistence in faith? Which needs more attention from you?

Worst (1) _____OK, but... _____ Best (10)

How do you think God would evaluate your leadership, including your support of leaders?

## QUESTIONS

1. Given Paul's comments in 1 Thessalonians 2:1–6, what rumors or untruths were his opponents circulating about him?

2. How can positive attitudes and honest communications by church members affect the perception by church leaders that they are supported and loved?

3. In light of this lesson's Scripture passage,
   what should your church do differently in the
   development and selection of church leaders?

4. Since "hard work" is a quality of good leaders, how
   can your church help leaders carry properly the
   burden of leadership without burning out?

NOTES ————————————————————————

1. See, for example, 1 Corinthians 9:5–15.

FOCAL TEXT
1 Thessalonians
4:1–12; 5:14–24

BACKGROUND
1 Thessalonians
4:1–12; 5:14–24

LESSON ELEVEN

# *Live to Please God and Win Others' Respect*

## MAIN IDEA

Christians are to live so as to both please God and win the respect of other people, especially people outside the church.

## QUESTION TO EXPLORE

How can we live distinctively as Christians and at the same time win the respect of people outside the church?

## STUDY AIM

To determine ways to live so as to please God and win the respect of other people, especially people outside the church

## QUICK READ

God is pleased when we aim to please him and live in right relationships with fellow Christians, but it does not end there. We must also relate to non-Christians in a way that wins their respect.

Athletes sometimes talk about whether they are getting respect. Some lament that their coaches do not appreciate their abilities or that opponents underestimate their skills. These assertions often occur after an impressive play turns the game around. Admiring themselves for what they have done, they are sure that others must see them in a new light. They think their critics will now have a higher opinion of them. So they feel *respected*, at least in their own eyes.

Reputation and respect are important. They reflect what others think of us. For Christians, that is an *inside-then-out* process. That is, our reputation is earned because of our character within. Character reflects who we really are; reputation deals with what other people think we are. Ideally who we are inside matches up with what others think of us. Our Scripture today speaks of winning the respect of people outside the church, but for Christians this is the result of a process that begins first with pleasing God.

# 1 THESSALONIANS 4:1–12

[1] Finally, brothers, we instructed you how to live in order to please God, as in fact you are living. Now we ask you and urge you in the Lord Jesus to do this more and more. [2] For you know what instructions we gave you by the authority of the Lord Jesus.

<sup>3</sup> It is God's will that you should be sanctified: that you should avoid sexual immorality; <sup>4</sup> that each of you should learn to control his own body in a way that is holy and honorable, <sup>5</sup> not in passionate lust like the heathen, who do not know God; <sup>6</sup> and that in this matter no one should wrong his brother or take advantage of him. The Lord will punish men for all such sins, as we have already told you and warned you. <sup>7</sup> For God did not call us to be impure, but to live a holy life. <sup>8</sup> Therefore, he who rejects this instruction does not reject man but God, who gives you his Holy Spirit.

<sup>9</sup> Now about brotherly love we do not need to write to you, for you yourselves have been taught by God to love each other. <sup>10</sup> And in fact, you do love all the brothers throughout Macedonia. Yet we urge you, brothers, to do so more and more.

<sup>11</sup> Make it your ambition to lead a quiet life, to mind your own business and to work with your hands, just as we told you, <sup>12</sup> so that your daily life may win the respect of outsiders and so that you will not be dependent on anybody.

# 1 THESSALONIANS 5:14–24

<sup>14</sup> And we urge you, brothers, warn those who are idle, encourage the timid, help the weak, be patient with everyone. <sup>15</sup> Make sure that nobody pays back wrong for

wrong, but always try to be kind to each other and to everyone else.

[16] Be joyful always; [17] pray continually; [18] give thanks in all circumstances, for this is God's will for you in Christ Jesus.

[19] Do not put out the Spirit's fire; [20] do not treat prophecies with contempt. [21] Test everything. Hold on to the good. [22] Avoid every kind of evil.

[23] May God himself, the God of peace, sanctify you through and through. May your whole spirit, soul and body be kept blameless at the coming of our Lord Jesus Christ. [24] The one who calls you is faithful and he will do it.

## Pleasing God (4:1–8)

*Radar-directed people* are very concerned about the opinions of others. They constantly scan the horizon, attempting to discern what others think of them. Often this type of personality is reflected in the workplace as someone appears to be working to solve a problem but is really more concerned about what others think of him or her while seeking a solution. This kind of scenario happens in churches as well.

When Paul was last with the Thessalonians, he made it a point to instruct them in how to live in order to please God. He stated that they were already living in this manner, but he urged them to be even more committed to this principle (1 Thessalonians 4:1). If your aim in life is to please God, then you open the door wider to all the good that God wants to do in your life. If your aim is to please others, then you open the door to only what other people can give you. When your main goal in life is to please others or to please only yourself, you will find that what you end up with is fool's gold.

The idea of holiness is behind the Greek word translated "sanctified" (1 Thess. 4:3; see also 4:7). Holiness is an important biblical theme. The root meaning of *holiness* is *different*. The Old Testament temple was holy because it was different from any other building. The Bible is holy because it is different from any other book. God's Spirit is holy because God's Spirit is different from any other spirit. Thus, Christians are holy because—how would you finish that sentence? Are we different from other people? Paul wrote that we should please God and to do this we are called "to live a holy life" (4:7).

"It is God's will that you should be sanctified" (4:3). This is the first sentence of the paragraph that calls us "to live a holy life." How does sanctification take place? Verse 8 mentions that God gives us his Holy Spirit. Is that the key? When we allow God's Spirit to control our lives, then we become what God intends us to be. We have no reason to be afraid of what God's Spirit will do to us. Paul summarized what God's Spirit wants to do in our lives in 2 Timothy 1:7: "God did not give us a spirit of timidity, but a spirit of power, of love and of self-discipline." Since that is what God wants to do in our lives, why don't we just accept God's will? Sanctification is more than just acceptance though; it is a joint venture of God's grace and our faith, God's offer and our acceptance, God's leadership and our following. Sanctification is God's command and our choice.

Between the commands to be "sanctified" in 4:3 and "to live a holy life" in 4:7, Paul focused on sexual immorality. The first century was steeped in sexual immorality, in part because a woman was considered a piece of property to be used at the whim of a man. In addition, moral standards were low during this time and the idea of sexual relations strictly within marriage was uncommon among the Gentiles. But under the Lordship of Jesus Christ and through the transforming power of the Holy Spirit, a new age dawned for those who repented and accepted Christ (see Acts 2). Paul stressed the importance of men and women leading a holy life, including avoiding sexual immorality. Although even Christians are not immune to temptation, sexuality is not an uncontrollable appetite but a godly gift that can be channeled so as to respect the personhood of all.

Paul told the Thessalonians to "control [your] own body in a way that is holy and honorable, not in passionate lust like the heathen" (1 Thess. 4:4–5). The non-Christian (or as Paul called them, "heathen") might act differently from Christians in many ways, but one sure sign of holiness in the first century was to not abuse or take advantage of people through sexual immorality. If Paul was here in the twenty-first century, do you think he would instruct us any differently? Don't forget, Paul was writing to church members, many of whom were young in the faith. What excuse do Christians have after twenty centuries of exposure to the Christian ethic and biblical instructions?

The call for a life that pleases God includes sanctification and holiness. Paul dealt with other holiness issues in chapter 5, but here he chose only one issue to make his point. When it comes to pleasing God, we must follow God's will in one of the most sensitive and special areas of life, human sexuality. Certainly there are other issues to consider—practicing racial prejudice, abusing one's power and position, lying, ignoring the poor, and the list goes on. Pleasing God applies to these matters and to many other areas as well.

Paul put this instruction about holiness in the context of the judgment of God. We can choose to please God or to please others—that's our choice. But, keep in mind that a time of accounting will come (4:6). Some today may have replaced the future judgment of God with merely looking good in the eyes of others, but the Bible is clear—we will each give an account of ourselves to God (Romans 14:12). I'm convinced that what God said of Jesus at his baptism is the same thing he would like to say about us—"I am well pleased" (Matthew 3:17).

## Love in the Church Family (4:9–10)

While I was eating lunch in a public place, a man sat down a few tables away from me. He was a resident of our city. The man with whom I was eating noticed the other man's arrival and began speaking harshly about him. I was surprised and chided him, "You shouldn't talk about him that way; he's your brother."

He said forcefully, "He's not my brother."

I said, "Yes he is; you go to the same church."

He paused but only for a moment. He retorted, "That may be so, but we don't sit on the same pew." Expletives have been deleted, but there were more than enough used that day to underscore his anger.

Like the Thessalonians, we have been taught the truth of the Scripture about love in the church family or, as it is usually translated, "brotherly love." We have probably heard many biblical and reasonable things in relation to this idea. For instance, since we are children of God, we are brothers and sisters in Christ. Or, children do not have the right to choose or reject brothers and sisters. We should all definitely recall one of the great commandments about loving our neighbor as ourselves (Matt. 22:39), or the new commandment of Jesus, to love one another as Jesus has loved us (John 13:34). If we thought about it, we probably could pile up an impressive list of Scripture on this topic. The bottom line, however, is that Christians often choose not to "sit on the same pew" with others while harboring resentment and dislike toward those who profess allegiance to the same Lord that we follow. Should that be so?

What Paul wrote to the Thessalonians, I simply say *amen* to and pass it along to you: "about brotherly love we do not need to write to you" (1 Thess. 4:9). But Paul continued to write anyway. The Thessalonians had a reputation for loving one another, and they expanded that circle throughout Macedonia. As with pleasing God, so too with brotherly love, Paul did not tell them to start practicing brotherly love. Rather he encouraged them to continue and grow in their love for one another "more and more" (4:10).

## Earn the Respect of Outsiders (4:11–12)

Paul continued with encouragement to live in such a way as to win the respect of outsiders. His appeal is evangelistic and practical. Through our good behavior, we can earn the respect of outsiders (see 1 Peter 3:15). Respect opens the door to many other witness and ministry opportunities. It may also remove doubts about the sincerity of our faith and behavior.

Keep the basic goal clear—our goal in life is not to win the respect of outsiders. Our goal is to please God. But when we do this the right way, we may win the respect of others as a bonus. As someone once said, "There is something wrong with every generalization, including this one." So you may find an exception to this idea about winning others' respect, but the general principle is still true. The best way to live is to please God. When we do, others may take notice of our behavior, and a positive change in their lives may result.

Verse 11 mentions the importance of leading a quiet life and working. Both actions are commendable. The Scripture also teaches, *MYOB*. Yes, "mind your own business" (1 Thess. 4:11). Apparently, even in the model church, some first-century Christians were meddlesome, perhaps even spreading half-truths and gossip. Can you imagine that taking place in church? A person giving the eulogy at his aunt's funeral said, "She probably used the phone in ways that Alexander Graham Bell never imagined." He was being kind about her ability to mind everyone else's business. Keep in mind that some things not only do not earn us respect, but they are entirely inappropriate for Christians.

## Further Evidence of a Holy Life (5:14–24)

Some see 5:14 as identifying four sources of problems in the Thessalonian church: the idlers, the fearful, the weak, and the immature. The church was encouraged to act in brotherly love to "warn those who are idle" (Paul later wrote: "if [you] will not work, [you] shall not eat,"

2 Thess. 3:10); "encourage the timid"; "help the weak"; and "be patient with everyone." We do not have certainty about the existence of these specific groups, but we do understand the verbs used in instruction: "warn"; "encourage"; "help"; and "be patient." Paul did all four of these while in Thessalonica. He wanted the church to continue to do the same even after he was gone. You likely have opportunities in which you could put these verbs to use yourself.

This section of Scripture contains many emphases. Some may call this a *buckshot* approach to teaching— scatter enough shot, and you'll hit something. What it seems to remind me of, however, is what I experienced each time I came home from college and then prepared to return. My mother would fill the last few minutes of our time with all kinds of advice and counsel. Perhaps it was her way of extending our time together, but I also think she wanted me to pay particular attention to those last things she said as I walked out the door. Paul had a lot to say and so little time and parchment left to do it, but these words are just as important as those that preceded them.

The following endnotes of Paul's are worthy of serious consideration, phrase by phrase. Take note of them for biblical assistance in working toward self-improvement.

- Don't try to get even with others; be kind (5:15).
- Rejoice, pray, and be thankful (5:16–18).

- Allow God's Spirit to run loose in your life (5:19).
- Use your mind to evaluate life so as to embrace good and reject evil (5:20–22).
- Claim Paul's prayer for the Thessalonians for yourself (5:23).
- Remember that God is faithful. God will help you become the person he wants you to be—a sanctified person who earns the respect of others.

## Taking It Personally

Christians are exceptional people. God has graced us with salvation, gifts, blessings, and opportunities. I'm constantly impressed by and thankful for all the good things that have come my way because of my relationship with Jesus Christ.

But we also can be exceptional in negative ways. We may think this is a good Scripture and a great lesson for somebody else. We may think our compromises do not matter much and the clear word of God about pleasing him and showing brotherly love is nice but does not apply to us. We may think we are the exceptions and it is not important for us to live in such a way that a non-believer may be attracted to Jesus. Even so, how we live our lives is always a reflection on the whole Christian community.

Think and pray about how you can be more intentional in pleasing God. Make a list of some people to whom you will make more of an effort to show Christian love. Find a specific way in which you can minister to someone, perhaps outside the traditional framework of the church, and make a positive impact as salt "of the earth" and light "of the world." On purpose, you can make a difference.

## HEROES OF THE FAITH

All heroes of the faith aren't famous or well-known. Harry left a significant business career to work for a Baptist children's home. Curtis carried tons of bread and other goods from the grocery store to the community food bank. Josephine delivered literature and visited shut-ins tirelessly. Hinson, a well-known public figure, called on church prospects in the toughest places of the city. Leona taught children at church for more than seventy years. Danny drooled and could not speak plainly, but his warm-hearted faithfulness inspired many. Emma and Mary Frances, like Dorcas in the Bible, were full of good works. These little-known Baptist heroes made a difference. Who are the heroes you know?

## ARE YOU GOING FURTHER WITH LOVE?

When it came to "brotherly love," Paul called the Thessalonian Christians "to do so more and more" (1 Thess. 4:9–10). Consider these possibilities for doing that today.

- *Family.* Pray for and reach out to family members who are estranged.

- *Church.* Intentionally seek to know other people better, especially across generational gaps.

- *Geographically.* Show your love for people who live far away from you.

- *Racially.* Reach across racial and cultural lines and genuinely love other people.

- *Your attitude.* Would anyone be attracted to the Christian faith because of your attitude?

## QUESTIONS

1. When Paul wrote about pleasing God, he said to do this more and more. If you did this, what effect would it have on your support of the church?

2. When Paul wrote about brotherly love, he said to show this more and more. If you showed this, what effect would it have on the people you know at church?

3. What attitudes and actions discussed in today's Scripture are displeasing to God?

4. What can your class do that shows you want to make a positive impact on outsiders?

LESSON TWELVE

# Hope for Time and Eternity

## MAIN IDEA

The hope Christ offers through his resurrection and promised return provides guidance and encouragement for life now and assurance for eternity.

## QUESTION TO EXPLORE

How does the hope Christ offers affect your life in both time and eternity?

## STUDY AIM

To put into my own words what the hope Christ offers means for my life now and as I consider eternity

## QUICK READ

Christ's resurrection and return enables us to deal positively with our grief as well as have hope for all eternity.

When I was about ten years old, an ambulance came to our neighbor's house. The father, in his mid-forties, died on the way to the hospital. About two years later, the ambulance came to our house. My father had a heart attack and was transported to the hospital. He survived and lived another thirty years, but there were other times in my life when I had to adjust to the new realization of the reality of death.

My experience with grief is common. We all deal with death and grief, but we do not need to walk alone. Our God is with us. Family and friends become encouragers, and the Scriptures become good medicine for aching hearts and troubled minds. We all "walk through the valley of the shadow of death" (Psalm 23:4), but that is not our permanent home.

The young converts in Thessalonica struggled with many issues. They did not have the New Testament for guidance, and the traveling apostles and teachers were not easily available to question. One issue in particular that the Thessalonians faced concerned the coming again of Christ. Some people misunderstood Paul and thought that all believers would live until Christ returned. So, when some died, they struggled with the implications this reality had for them. Paul addressed their concern in 1 Thessalonians, and then he wrote again on the subject in 2 Thessalonians. Now, 2,000 years later, we still realize that there is more that we *don't* know about Christ's Second Coming than we do. However, we know enough to have hope and assurance.

# 1 THESSALONIANS 4:13–18

**13** Brothers, we do not want you to be ignorant about those who fall asleep, or to grieve like the rest of men, who have no hope. **14** We believe that Jesus died and rose again and so we believe that God will bring with Jesus those who have fallen asleep in him. **15** According to the Lord's own word, we tell you that we who are still alive, who are left till the coming of the Lord, will certainly not precede those who have fallen asleep. **16** For the Lord himself will come down from heaven, with a loud command, with the voice of the archangel and with the trumpet call of God, and the dead in Christ will rise first. **17** After that, we who are still alive and are left will be caught up together with them in the clouds to meet the Lord in the air. And so we will be with the Lord forever. **18** Therefore encourage each other with these words.

# 1 THESSALONIANS 5:1–11

**1** Now, brothers, about times and dates we do not need to write to you, **2** for you know very well that the day of the Lord will come like a thief in the night. **3** While people are saying, "Peace and safety," destruction will come on them suddenly, as labor pains on a pregnant woman, and they will not escape.

**4** But you, brothers, are not in darkness so that this day should surprise you like a thief. **5** You are all sons of the light and sons of the day. We do not belong to the night or to the darkness. **6** So then, let us not be like others, who are asleep, but let us be alert and self-controlled. **7** For those who sleep, sleep at night, and those who get drunk, get drunk at night. **8** But since we belong to the day, let us be self-controlled, putting on faith and love as a breastplate, and the hope of salvation as a helmet. **9** For God did not appoint us to suffer wrath but to receive salvation through our Lord Jesus Christ. **10** He died for us so that, whether we are awake or asleep, we may live together with him. **11** Therefore encourage one another and build each other up, just as in fact you are doing.

## Ignorance, Grief, and Hope (4:13–18)

Death is one of life's common denominators. Unless the Lord returns first, we all will die. So will our loved ones and friends. That is the obvious reality. The Thessalonians knew this truth, but they had questions. What is the fate of our loved ones who have already died? Will Christ return soon? Has Christ already come and we have missed it? Keep in mind that the Thessalonian Christians to whom Paul wrote lived about twenty years after the death, resurrection, and ascension of Jesus. The thought of Jesus' coming again was fresh in their minds.

*Ignorance* literally means *not knowing*. We do not know some things simply because we lack the required information. Other things are not within our ability to grasp completely; they are simply too mysterious. Failing to understand mysteries does not indicate a lack of intelligence, and neither is it a sign of moral weakness. We just have to accept the fact that we will never know everything. When it comes to the Second Coming, we have information that allows us to be aware of this truth, but since we don't have all the answers, it remains a mystery.

We use the word *ignore* when someone knows but disregards the truth. That was not the problem with the Thessalonians. They were not ignoring the truth. Rather, they did not know or understand the entire truth. Therefore, they asked for more clarification. Paul did not berate them for asking or not knowing. It's okay to ask questions of God or others in your search for truth and understanding.

Paul did not want the church to be ignorant, and neither did he want them to grieve as people without hope. That's one thing grief can do to us. It sometimes robs us of our hope, or at least, it makes us think for a while that we are hopeless and helpless. Paul cited the coming again of Christ as a primary reason for the hope we can have during times of grief.

A pastor search committee was interviewing a friend of mine. They really liked him as a prospective pastor for their church. Discussion about the Second Coming was a hot subject in their church. Finally, a committee member popped the question. "Pastor, what is your opinion on the Second Coming of Jesus? Are you a *pre, post* or *a* millennialist?"

My friend answered, "I am a *pro*-millennialist. Whenever God wants to do it, I'm for it." That seemed to break the tension. My friend was called to serve that church, and he spent several years of meaningful ministry with the congregation.

People view history in many different ways. Some think history moves in cycles, repeating itself with a different set of characters. Some think life is meaningless, just a headache between two zeroes. Others see peaks and valleys, knowing that we can learn from each and we can see progress. However, to them, nothing is unique about the influence of religious tradition throughout history. The Christian perspective, however, embraces history as *HIS*-story. For the Christian faith, history has a beginning point with God and is moving toward a conclusion, when Christ will return and the entire universe will be changed. Those who have believed in Jesus Christ as Savior and Lord will spend eternity with him. Life has a purpose, and the events of history lead toward a goal.

We find no biblical *if* about Christ's return, only *when*—and *when* is not for us to know. Paul gave some particulars in 1 Thessalonians 4:14–17 regarding the concern of the Thessalonians for those who had died and for those who were still alive. His words assure us that God has taken care of those who have died and that God will take care of those still alive when Jesus comes. The

Lord will return, and the Lord's return will be obvious to believers and non-believers alike.

Paul closed this section with these words: "So we will be with the Lord forever. Therefore encourage each other with these words" (1 Thessalonians 4:17–18). It takes only a few seconds to read those words, but their meaning is awesome. Jesus promised his disciples he would come again. He also said we, as believers, would share eternity with him. For the Thessalonians and for us, we can be encouraged to know that history is moving toward a goal and that one day, we will be with the Lord forever. Life is more than being born, living a few years, and then dying. We who follow Jesus have the presence of God with us now, and, when we die, we know we will be with God forever. What a hope for us and for our loved ones!

Yes, we grieve when we lose loved ones. That's normal. If we lose an item we value, we will usually search diligently for it. Losing the continuous fellowship with loved ones is an even greater loss. But searching for them will not bring them back. However, we can move forward with our lives, knowing that God has taken care of our loved ones and will continue to take care of us.

The story of the death of Lazarus in John 11 is instructive. Jesus was told about Lazarus's illness and death, but it was several days before he showed up at the home of Lazarus and his sisters, Mary and Martha. Both sisters chastised Jesus for not coming sooner. They believed that if Jesus had arrived earlier, then Lazarus would not have died. The Scripture tells us that when Jesus saw the grief of those who were there, "Jesus wept" (John 11:35). Even Jesus felt the burden of grief and shed tears over the loss of a friend. Of course, Jesus then showed all those gathered the glory of God when he called Lazarus to come out of his tomb. This miracle foreshadows what God will eventually do for all believers. Although believers die, we do not die eternally. "So we will be with the Lord forever" (1 Thess. 4:17). These words comfort us.

## Coming Again (5:1–11)

Some years ago, in 1977, my wife and I were in London, England. Our guide led us through the magnificent city, pointing out the historical significance of one place after another. At one point, she paused in her history to tell us about the cleanliness of the city. Coal smoke stains had been removed from buildings, and much care had been given to make the city beautiful. She explained that in a few months, England would celebrate the twenty-fifth anniversary of the coronation of Queen Elizabeth. She said, "We're getting ready for the coming of the Queen."

As Christians, we are looking forward to another kind of coming—the return of the King. The Thessalonians had been assured that Christ's return was still in the future, but when it happened, they would know it. In 5:1, Paul echoed what Jesus said in Matthew 24:36 and Acts

1:6–8—we do not know when this will take place. Even Jesus, in his humanness, said he did not know; only the Father knows.

Over the years, various individuals have chosen dates and insisted that the Lord would return on those dates. They were obviously wrong; others who pick dates in the future for Christ's return will also be wrong. Many people have taught and preached as if they had some strong knowledge that the Lord was coming soon, perhaps even by a specific date. If they were right and so sure of this, why did they then end their broadcast by asking for money? If Jesus really was returning on the date they announced, why would they have had a need for money?

The phrase "day of the Lord" (5:2) refers to our Lord's return. For Christians, we have nothing to fear; it will be a stunning and glorious day. The anticipation of such a time encourages us to have hope for all the time that remains. On the other hand, for those who have opposed the work of God and are not believers, that day will also be stunning but definitely not glorious, as destruction will come on them.

Peter addressed the Second Coming similarly. He wrote, "Since everything will be destroyed in this way, what kind of people ought you to be?" (2 Pet. 3:11). In the same verse, he answered his own question: "You ought to live holy and godly lives." Paul would have answered the question in similar fashion.

Paul used various words and phrases in these verses to describe how we should live in light of Christ's return.

- We are to be "alert and self-controlled" (1 Thess. 5:6).
- We are to live with "faith," "love," and "hope" (5:8).
- We are to "encourage one another and build each other up, just as in fact you are doing" (5:11; see 4:18).

Paul's last words in verse 11 ("in fact you are doing") indicate again the quality of the church at Thessalonica. Paul taught them to encourage one another and build one another up. That's what Christians can do for one another as they wait for the Second Coming. One of Paul's missionary companions was Barnabas. His name meant "Son of Encouragement" (Acts 4:36). All of us can be like Barnabas—encouraging and building people up. Whatever our ignorance or whatever our pain, Christians encourage and build up others.

## Taking It Personally

My older brother died in a plane wreck some years ago. He left his wife and five children, ages three to fourteen. A few months afterward, I was in the front yard with my father. A friend stopped by and asked, "Joe, how are you getting over it?"

My father replied, "I don't think I will get over it, but I'm able to deal with it a little better each day or so." We all go through the different stages of grief, but there is no set time line that fits every person.

We grieve for our loss, but still we have hope. The knowledge that our Lord is coming again and that life has a purpose and a goal not only produce hopes but is the result of hope. Surely, we can comfort one another with words and knowledge, as our Scripture suggests. Words, however, are heard best from the mouths of people who genuinely care for one another.

In 2 Corinthians 1:3–4 Paul mentioned a cycle of comfort: we need comfort; God comforts us; then we use that comfort to comfort others. Don't waste the peace and knowledge you have of life and death, grief and comfort. Share it with others. We all have pockets of ignorance; none of us has all the answers. But what we all can foster is a caring disposition that allows us to act on behalf of the welfare of others. Who knows, you may be the answer to someone's prayer today.

## A Caution on "Second Coming" Study

A college student told me about a retreat he was going to attend during spring break. I asked him whether there was a study theme for the retreat. He said, "Yes, we are studying Revelation. We've studied it before, but I'm going to get it down pat this time." I appreciated his zeal, but I cautioned him, replying, "Getting Revelation down pat is like dividing three into ten. There's always something left over."

As you consider the Second Coming of Christ, let it encourage you. That was Paul's purpose in writing about it. Do not become obsessed with getting all the particulars and different Scriptures "down pat." Be aware that in seeking to understand complex subjects characterized by symbolic language and mystery, we can fall victim to a *cut-and-paste* approach to the Bible. In this approach, we try to synchronize Scripture to make everything fit the way we think it should. A scheme of *cutting and pasting* can take priority over letting Scripture speak for itself. *Getting it down pat* may lead people to reconstruct the Bible according to their opinion or the opinion of some previous reconstructionist, rather than letting their opinion be shaped by the Bible.

## DEALING WITH GRIEF

When the wife of a Baptist leader died, a friend went to comfort him and said, "I'm sorry you lost your wife." The man replied, "My wife is not lost; I know where she is. I'm the one who's lost." What do you think he meant by that? Do you know anyone now who might feel this same way?

## QUESTIONS ————————————————————

1. How does this Scripture passage help you deal with any fears you may have about your own death?

2. What part can you play in helping your church minister to those who grieve?

3. When a person feels hopeless, what attitudes and behaviors may develop?

4. How do God's plans for you in 1 Thessalonians 5:9–11 affect your attitude and behavior?

5. If you could improve one trait of yours, based on a study of this lesson, what would that be and how would you accomplish it?

6. What are you ignorant about? What can you do to seek more knowledge and understanding?

LESSON THIRTEEN

# Being a Thriving Church in a Tough Situation

## MAIN IDEA

Being a thriving church in a tough situation calls for relying on God's strength and the support of one's fellow believers; being faithful in one's daily life, including at work; and following Christian teachings.

## QUESTION TO EXPLORE

What does being a thriving church in a tough situation require?

## STUDY AIM

To consider how I can help my church become a thriving church

## QUICK READ

Churches can thrive in tough circumstances. Thriving churches depend on the power of God and the faithfulness of its members to do the right thing.

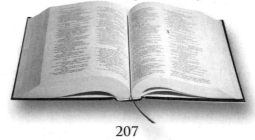

Operation Andrew was an outreach effort by our church in which we encouraged our members to identify ten people who were not Christians or were not active in a church. They committed to pray for these people and asked God to open doors so they could witness to them. Many made this commitment, but one was extra special to me.

An elderly member called and said she did not have the physical ability to visit people anymore and did not know many unchurched people. Still, she wanted to be part of Operation Andrew. She said she could pray for ten people if I would send her a list of names. I was happy to mail her a list. About three months later, she called again. She asked me if she could have a new list. She said, "Nine on my list made decisions at church, and one moved away!" Not all stories had such a happy report, but here was direct evidence of the value of our church's praying for people.

## 2 THESSALONIANS 3:1–16

¹ Finally, brothers, pray for us that the message of the Lord may spread rapidly and be honored, just as it was with you. ² And pray that we may be delivered from wicked and evil men, for not everyone has faith. ³ But the Lord is faithful, and he will strengthen and protect you from the evil

one. **4** We have confidence in the Lord that you are doing and will continue to do the things we command. **5** May the Lord direct your hearts into God's love and Christ's perseverance.

**6** In the name of the Lord Jesus Christ, we command you, brothers, to keep away from every brother who is idle and does not live according to the teaching you received from us. **7** For you yourselves know how you ought to follow our example. We were not idle when we were with you, **8** nor did we eat anyone's food without paying for it. On the contrary, we worked night and day, laboring and toiling so that we would not be a burden to any of you. **9** We did this, not because we do not have the right to such help, but in order to make ourselves a model for you to follow. **10** For even when we were with you, we gave you this rule: "If a man will not work, he shall not eat."

**11** We hear that some among you are idle. They are not busy; they are busybodies. **12** Such people we command and urge in the Lord Jesus Christ to settle down and earn the bread they eat. **13** And as for you, brothers, never tire of doing what is right.

**14** If anyone does not obey our instruction in this letter, take special note of him. Do not associate with him, in order that he may feel ashamed. **15** Yet do not regard him as an enemy, but warn him as a brother.

**16** Now may the Lord of peace himself give you peace at all times and in every way. The Lord be with all of you.

## Thriving Churches Pray (3:1–5)

In the Old Testament, Israel got their wish when they asked for a king, but in the end, they did not like what they got. In a contrite spirit, they went to the prophet Samuel for wisdom. They asked him to pray for them. Note part of Samuel's response to their prayer request: "far be it from me that I should sin against the LORD by failing to pray for you" (1 Samuel 12:23). That puts prayer into a different context, doesn't it? Samuel believed that if he failed to pray for the Israelites, he was sinning against God. Have you ever considered the failure to pray for one another to be a sin against God?

In more than one letter, Paul asked people to pray for him. Paul knew himself better than anyone else did. He knew his strengths, and he knew his limitations. Above all, he knew that God had called him to a special ministry, but he needed to live a life that was totally devoted to God in order to achieve the purpose God had given him. Paul did not toss the request for prayer casually into his letters. His prayer request acknowledged his dependence on the power of God and his belief in the power of intercessory prayer.

As far as we know, the Thessalonians prayed for him. Paul's ministry may have lasted another fifteen years after he wrote to the Thessalonians. How many people prayed for him? How much was accomplished through their prayers? No one knows that answer, but every minister I know would not want to try to serve without the prayerful support of fellow believers.

Paul's prayer request was twofold (2 Thessalonians 3:1–2). His first prayer request was that the gospel would move like wildfire and would be widely accepted. Second, he asked that the Thessalonians would pray that Silas, Timothy, and he would be delivered from "wicked and evil" people. Paul was harassed constantly by people similar to what he used to be! These people, called Judaizers by some, often used non-Jewish public officials to cause problems for Paul.

Paul knew that "not everyone has faith" (2 Thess. 3:2). That realism must have caused sorrow in his soul. As he wrote to the church at Rome, "my heart's desire and prayer to God for the Israelites is that they may be saved" (Romans 10:1). But, the critics did not have faith, and they hounded Paul. He referred to them as "wicked and evil men."

This reference to not everyone having faith may also have been about another group. One thing early churches faced was the infiltration of their fellowship by unscrupulous people. They posed as believers and may even have become teachers. Then, though, they caused many problems within the church. Even in the model church at Thessalonica, some people were probably not true believers. Paul prayed for deliverance, regardless of the source.

Paul's prayer request led him to describe one of the qualities of God: faithfulness (1 Thess. 3:3). God is faithful.

Those three words ring out through the entire Bible. God is faithful. Paul was sure that the people's prayer to God on his behalf would make a difference to him. He also was confident that what he asked for himself, God would do for them also: "he will strengthen and protect you from the evil one" (3:3).

Jesus taught the model prayer, which included "deliver us from evil" (Matthew 6:13, KJV). Some translations say "from the evil one" (NIV, NRSV). The larger struggle in life was not just between Paul and his antagonists. Then and now, a cosmic struggle is taking place every day that represents the power of the evil one to corrupt and destroy. The good news is that the power of evil to ruin is not greater than the power of God to save and empower. Evil and the evil one can be resisted, although it is not in our power to banish it from earth. God will do that in the end. Until then, Paul's confidence was that his faithful God would "strengthen and protect" the Thessalonians.

Paul had confidence in the Thessalonians as well (1 Thess. 3:4). He commended them in both of the Thessalonian letters. Paul wrote some things that they should do and he believed they would do them. Let us give Paul the apostolic power granted to him. Paul's words are not just good advice or suggestions. Here he called them commands.

Paul continued to pray that the Lord would direct the "hearts" of the Thessalonians, that they would (1) grow deeper in the love of God and (2) have perseverance (3:5). Our identity as believers is secure in that we are God's children and God loves us. Our lives are compelled by love that is from God and like God. "We love because he first loved us" (1 John 4:19). That love enables us to keep going. We need to recognize the importance of perseverance, or endurance. Sometimes, in tough places, we need to put our heads down and push forward rather than falling back on the cliché of "when one door closes, another door opens." Don't forget that Satan is trying to close doors of opportunity. What Paul prayed for the Thessalonians is also a prayer for you and me: we are loved by God; don't quit or waver.

## Thriving Churches Work (3:6–15)

As we noted in lesson twelve, one issue that troubled the Thessalonians was the Second Coming. Some may have thought that the Lord was coming soon, literally *soon*. This may have led to Paul's testimony that he worked hard among them (1 Thess. 2:9) and he instructed them to work also (4:11). Some New Testament scholars see a direct relationship between these two matters in the church: people expected the Lord to return soon, and so they quit working to wait. Whether this interpretation is appropriate, that their idleness followed from their perspective on the Second Coming, is uncertain. Even so,

Paul was led to devote considerable attention to idleness and the need, for those who were able, to work.

The early church practiced what we might call *communalism*, as we read in Acts 4:32: "No one claimed that any of his possessions was his own, but they shared everything they had." We have little evidence of how widespread this practice was or how long it lasted. Even so, the early church made a significant point of caring for one another; to do this well would have involved sacrifice and ministry by many people. If some sort of communalism was going on in Thessalonica, then Paul's teaching about work, including his famous line of "if a man will not work, he shall not eat" (3:10) takes on more meaning. Even we who enjoy potluck suppers would not think very highly of people who came to eat but never brought a pot and were well able to do so!

Paul's devotion to work is a serious matter. Apparently some of the people were "idle," and in that state they became "busybodies" (2 Thess. 3:11). "An idle mind is the devil's workshop," so we have been told. Whoever these people were at Thessalonica, their idleness and meddlesomeness disrupted the church. Paul advised two things about them: (1) don't hang out with them (3:6); and (2) don't treat them as an enemy but regard them and warn them as a brother (3:15). Apparently, Paul had not given up on the idlers even though he was very upset with them.

These idlers did not learn their behavior from Paul. Just as in his first letter, Paul pointed out again how he worked night and day among the Thessalonians. He worked hard and provided them with a good example. If anyone were tempted to follow the example of the idlers, Paul's teaching is abundantly plain. Don't become like the lazy and idle.

Paul pointed out that the Thessalonians should never tire of doing the right thing. This included taking care of those who might have been unable to work; Paul's many other teachings would cover what was to be done in those circumstances. The early church cared for those less fortunate. As Paul wrote to the Galatians, "As we have opportunity, let us do good to all people, especially to those who belong to the family of believers" (Gal. 6:10). The need continues for the church to find ways to take better care of one another as well as to reach out in ministry to those outside the church.


## Thriving Churches Are Peaceful (3:16)

The church sign was easy to read, "Welcome to Harmony Baptist Church." A few miles farther, another sign was posted: "Welcome to New Harmony Baptist Church." Something happened to harmony among the Baptists.

The Beatitudes of Jesus are attitudes that need to be in our lives. Jesus said, "Blessed are the peacemakers, for they will be called the sons of God" (Matt. 5:9). How are we known among believers and among non-Christians?

Could other people guess that we are children of God because we are such peaceable people?

Christians can become unhappy with one another in the best of churches, even in a model church like Thessalonica. Paul's prayerful last thoughts for this good church were that they be people who were united and at peace with one another. The progression of thought in this verse is simple. Our God is "the Lord of peace." Paul prayed that God's peace would dominate every circumstance and every person. He also prayed that the Lord would be with all of them. In reality, God already promised this to his people. In writing it, Paul may have taken one last opportunity to remind the church about what really makes the church—the presence of God in each and all of them. If we respected that fact more, perhaps we would demonstrate greater peace.

Most churches want to thrive and grow. One of the greatest keys to evangelism and church growth is genuine love and fellowship. When we love one another as God has loved us, people can hear and see the gospel in our lives. When we are kind and forgiving, people catch the spirit and want to be part of it. When we move forward together in bold commitment to God, newcomers want to join in. Living in peace not only makes evangelism more likely, but it also makes our church experience more enjoyable.

When our children were younger, I once watched as the three of them pushed away from the dock and paddled a boat across the cove of a large lake. You can probably guess how well three children (ages thirteen, ten, and seven) did with three paddles. It was a hoot! They went in circles, they hollered for help, and they blamed each other. Finally, they worked together long enough to get back to the dock. When you paddle a small boat with an odd number of people, it really helps to be united around a common plan and purpose. That's a good idea for churches as well, for we too may be an odd number of people!

## Taking It Personally

A remarkable fact of church history is that this model church existed in difficult circumstances. We focused in this study on just three positive qualities, but we have seen so many more in the previous studies. The Thessalonian Christians were committed to God and one another. Their lives exhibited faith, hope, love, endurance, prayerfulness, hard work, peace, and so much more. They did not allow circumstances or a hostile environment to govern their experience. They thrived.

If one church thrives, can every church thrive? That depends on what it means to thrive. Do budgets, baptisms, and buildings prove that a church is thriving, plateauing, or weakening? We could argue those points, but most of us want our churches to thrive by being places of faith and love where others come to build or strengthen a relationship with the Lord.

What if your church circumstances change for the worse? We could *what if* many options, but we have no need to walk under a cloud of doom. The bottom line is: we can unite to pray, plan, and work to see that our church is faithful to the purpose God has for us. Could you commit yourself to that?

## CHURCH DISCIPLINE

Paul wrote about people who needed to be disciplined; however, he reminded the Thessalonians that they were fellow Christians also (2 Thess. 3:15). In another discipline case in Galatians 6, the teaching was to restore people with gentleness and to be sensitive to one's own weaknesses.

Some have joked that the Baptist ethic of earlier years was *I don't dance, drink, smoke, or chew, or run around with girls who do.* Church discipline from those days tended to focus on issues such as these, while ignoring others like pride, greed, exploitation of the poor, racial and gender discrimination, and a host of other sins.

Church discipline can be positive, and positive church discipline begins at the front door. Baptizing people without discipling them often leaves them only wet. Discipleship can start before conversion, but it needs to accelerate after conversion. People need to learn about blessings and responsibilities, gifts and opportunities. The church should love people through the hard times, lovingly giving correction as needed. Although we may not practice church discipline like Paul used at Thessalonica or as our ancestors did, we can model disciplined lives and try to help all believers grow in their relationship with Christ and the mission of the church.

## STEPPING UP

In athletics, when a star player is injured, a substitute steps up and often does a great job, taking advantage of an opportunity to shine. In churches, we do not have stars, but you have probably heard the idea that twenty percent of the people do eighty percent of the work.

Let's say you are the new recruitment minister. Your job is to develop policy and then to recruit and train volunteers to staff several new ministries as well as the traditional positions in the church. What leadership and personal qualities have you found in the Thessalonian letters that will be helpful to your new ministry? How can you help people agree to step up and serve effectively?

## QUESTIONS

1. If your church wrote a plan to thrive, what would you include?

2. If Paul's teaching about work were applied to volunteer work within the church, how would your church be affected?

3. If children learned from your example as the Thessalonians did from Paul, what would they learn about prayer, work, and peace?

4. What can you encourage your church to do to be more sensitive to those who want to work but cannot?

5. What should churches do about members who may not talk negatively about the church but have shown no interest in being a part of church life?

# Our Next New Study

(Available for use beginning December 2009)

# THE GOSPEL OF LUKE:
## Good News of Great Joy

*This special eighteen-session study of the Gospel of Luke provides guidance for studying Jesus' life and ministry from Christmas to Easter.*

### UNIT ONE: JESUS' BIRTH AND CHILDHOOD

### UNIT TWO: PREPARING FOR MINISTRY

## UNIT THREE: JESUS' MINISTRY IN GALILEE

Lesson 8    Fulfilled Today?                                     Luke 4:14–21
Lesson 9    Jesus' Radical Message                               Luke 4:22–30
Lesson 10   Called to Gather People for the Kingdom   Luke 5:1–11
Lesson 11   Jesus' Life-Altering Instructions                    Luke 6:17–46
Lesson 12   Where Forgiveness Leads                              Luke 7:36–50

## UNIT FOUR: JOURNEYING TO JERUSALEM

Lesson 13   A Narrow Door, a Limited Time          Luke 13:22–35
Lesson 14   Priority Matters                                   Luke 14:1–24
Lesson 15   Coming to the Party?                               Luke 15:1–2, 8–32
Lesson 16   A Fatal Mistake                                    Luke 16:19–31

## UNIT FIVE: JESUS' DEATH AND RESURRECTION

Lesson 17   Crucified—for Us                  Luke 23:1–26, 32–49
Lesson 18   Resurrected—for Us                Luke 24:1–10, 33–39, 44–48

Additional Resources for Studying the *Gospel of Luke: Good News of Great Joy*[1]

Darrell L. Bock. *The NIV Application Commentary: Luke.* Grand Rapids, Michigan: Zondervan Publishing House, 1996.

Fred B. Craddock. *Luke.* Interpretation: A Bible Commentary for Teaching and Preaching. Louisville, Kentucky: John Knox Press, 1990.

R. Alan Culpepper, "The Gospel of Luke." *The New Interpreter's Bible.* Volume 9. Nashville: Abingdon Press, 1995.

Craig S. Keener. *IVP Bible Background Commentary: New Testament.* Downers Grove, Illinois: InterVarsity Press, 1993.

A.T. Robertson. *Word Pictures in the New Testament.* Volume II. The Gospel of Luke. Nashville, Tennessee: Broadman Press, 1930.

Charles H. Talbert. *Reading Luke: A Literary and Theological Commentary.* Revised edition. Macon, Georgia: Smyth & Helwys Publishing, Inc., 2002.

Malcolm Tolbert. "Luke." *The Broadman Bible Commentary.* Volume 9. Nashville: Broadman Press, 1970.

## Additional Future Adult Bible Studies

| | |
|---|---|
| *Genesis: People Relating to God* | For use beginning April 11, 2010 |
| (NOTE: This study of Genesis is an 8-session study.) | |
| *Living Faith in Daily Life* | For use beginning June 2010 |
| *Letters of James, Peter, and John* | For use beginning September 2010 |

NOTES

1. Listing a book does not imply full agreement by the writers or BAPTISTWAY PRESS® with all of its comments.

# How to Order More Bible Study Materials

It's easy! Just fill in the following information. For additional Bible study materials, see www.baptistwaypress.org or get a complete order form of available materials by calling 1-866-249-1799 or e-mailing baptistway@bgct.org.

| Title of item | Price | Quantity | Cost |
|---|---|---|---|
| **This Issue:** | | | |
| Galatians and 1&2 Thessalonians—Study Guide (BWP001080) | $3.55 | | |
| Galatians and 1&2 Thessalonians—Large Print Study Guide (BWP001081) | $3.95 | | |
| Galatians and 1&2 Thessalonians—Teaching Guide (BWP001082) | $3.95 | | |
| **Additional Issues Available:** | | | |
| Growing Together in Christ—Study Guide (BWP001036) | $3.25 | | |
| Growing Together in Christ—Large Print Study Guide (BWP001037) | $3.55 | | |
| Growing Together in Christ—Teaching Guide (BWP001038) | $3.75 | | |
| Participating in God's Mission—Study Guide (BWP001077) | $3.55 | | |
| Participating in God's Mission—Large Print Study Guide (BWP001078) | $3.95 | | |
| Participating in God's Mission—Teaching Guide (BWP001079) | $3.95 | | |
| Genesis 12—50: Family Matters—Study Guide (BWP000034) | $1.95 | | |
| Genesis 12—50: Family Matters—Teaching Guide (BWP000035) | $2.45 | | |
| Leviticus, Numbers, Deuteronomy—Study Guide (BWP000053) | $2.35 | | |
| Leviticus, Numbers, Deuteronomy—Large Print Study Guide (BWP000052) | $2.35 | | |
| Leviticus, Numbers, Deuteronomy—Teaching Guide (BWP000054) | $2.95 | | |
| Joshua, Judges—Study Guide (BWP000047) | $2.35 | | |
| Joshua, Judges—Large Print Study Guide (BWP000046) | $2.35 | | |
| Joshua, Judges—Teaching Guide (BWP000048) | $2.95 | | |
| 1 and 2 Samuel—Study Guide (BWP000002) | $2.35 | | |
| 1 and 2 Samuel—Large Print Study Guide (BWP000001) | $2.35 | | |
| 1 and 2 Samuel—Teaching Guide (BWP000003) | $2.95 | | |
| 1 and 2 Kings: Leaders and Followers—Study Guide (BWP001025) | $2.95 | | |
| 1 and 2 Kings: Leaders and Followers Large Print Study Guide (BWP001026) | $3.15 | | |
| 1 and 2 Kings: Leaders and Followers Teaching Guide (BWP001027) | $3.45 | | |
| Ezra, Haggai, Zechariah, Nehemiah, Malachi—Study Guide (BWP001071) | $3.25 | | |
| Ezra, Haggai, Zechariah, Nehemiah, Malachi—Large Print Study Guide (BWP001072) | $3.55 | | |
| Ezra, Haggai, Zechariah, Nehemiah, Malachi—Teaching Guide (BWP001073) | $3.75 | | |
| Job, Ecclesiastes, Habakkuk, Lamentations—Study Guide (BWP001016) | $2.75 | | |
| Job, Ecclesiastes, Habakkuk, Lamentations—Large Print Study Guide (BWP001017) | $2.85 | | |
| Job, Ecclesiastes, Habakkuk, Lamentations—Teaching Guide (BWP001018) | $3.25 | | |
| Psalms and Proverbs—Study Guide (BWP001000) | $2.75 | | |
| Psalms and Proverbs—Large Print Study Guide (BWP001001) | $2.85 | | |
| Psalms and Proverbs—Teaching Guide (BWP001002) | $3.25 | | |
| Matthew: Hope in the Resurrected Christ—Study Guide (BWP001066) | $3.25 | | |
| Matthew: Hope in the Resurrected Christ—Large Print Study Guide (BWP001067) | $3.55 | | |
| Matthew: Hope in the Resurrected Christ—Teaching Guide (BWP001068) | $3.75 | | |
| Mark: Jesus' Works and Words—Study Guide (BWP001022) | $2.95 | | |
| Mark: Jesus' Works and Words—Large Print Study Guide (BWP001023) | $3.15 | | |
| Mark:Jesus' Works and Words—Teaching Guide (BWP001024) | $3.45 | | |
| Jesus in the Gospel of Mark—Study Guide (BWP000066) | $1.95 | | |
| Jesus in the Gospel of Mark—Large Print Study Guide (BWP000065) | $1.95 | | |
| Jesus in the Gospel of Mark—Teaching Guide (BWP000067) | $2.45 | | |
| Luke: Journeying to the Cross—Study Guide (BWP000057) | $2.35 | | |
| Luke: Journeying to the Cross—Large Print Study Guide (BWP000056) | $2.35 | | |
| Luke: Journeying to the Cross—Teaching Guide (BWP000058) | $2.95 | | |
| The Gospel of John: The Word Became Flesh—Study Guide (BWP001008) | $2.75 | | |
| The Gospel of John: The Word Became Flesh—Large Print Study Guide (BWP001009) | $2.85 | | |
| The Gospel of John: The Word Became Flesh—Teaching Guide (BWP001010) | $3.25 | | |
| Acts: Toward Being a Missional Church—Study Guide (BWP001013) | $2.75 | | |
| Acts: Toward Being a Missional Church—Large Print Study Guide (BWP001014) | $2.85 | | |
| Acts: Toward Being a Missional Church—Teaching Guide (BWP001015) | $3.25 | | |
| Romans: What God Is Up To—Study Guide (BWP001019) | $2.95 | | |
| Romans: What God Is Up To—Large Print Study Guide (BWP001020) | $3.15 | | |
| Romans: What God Is Up To—Teaching Guide (BWP001021) | $3.45 | | |

| | | |
|---|---|---|
| Ephesians, Philippians, Colossians—*Study Guide* (BWP001060) | $3.25 | _____  _____ |
| Ephesians, Philippians, Colossians—*Large Print Study Guide* (BWP001061) | $3.55 | _____  _____ |
| Ephesians, Philippians, Colossians—*Teaching Guide* (BWP001062) | $3.75 | _____  _____ |
| 1, 2 Timothy, Titus, Philemon—*Study Guide* (BWP000092) | $2.75 | _____  _____ |
| 1, 2 Timothy, Titus, Philemon—*Large Print Study Guide* (BWP000091) | $2.85 | _____  _____ |
| 1, 2 Timothy, Titus, Philemon—*Teaching Guide* (BWP000093) | $3.25 | _____  _____ |
| Revelation—*Study Guide* (BWP000084) | $2.35 | _____  _____ |
| Revelation—*Large Print Study Guide* (BWP000083) | $2.35 | _____  _____ |
| Revelation—*Teaching Guide* (BWP000085) | $2.95 | _____  _____ |

## Coming for use beginning December 2009

(a special 18-session study from Christmas to Easter: the price of the study reflects the additional number of lessons)

| | | |
|---|---|---|
| The Gospel of Luke—*Study Guide* (BWP001085) | $4.90 | _____  _____ |
| The Gospel of Luke—*Large Print Study Guide* (BWP001086) | $5.45 | _____  _____ |
| The Gospel of Luke—*Teaching Guide* (BWP001087) | $5.45 | _____  _____ |

| Standard (UPS/Mail) Shipping Charges* | | | |
|---|---|---|---|
| Order Value | Shipping charge** | Order Value | Shipping charge** |
| $.01—$9.99 | $6.50 | $160.00—$199.99 | $22.00 |
| $10.00—$19.99 | $8.00 | $200.00—$249.99 | $26.00 |
| $20.00—$39.99 | $9.00 | $250.00—$299.99 | $28.00 |
| $40.00—$59.99 | $10.00 | $300.00—$349.99 | $32.00 |
| $60.00—$79.99 | $11.00 | $350.00—$399.99 | $40.00 |
| $80.00—$99.99 | $12.00 | $400.00—$499.99 | $48.00 |
| $100.00—$129.99 | $14.00 | $500.00—$599.99 | $58.00 |
| $130.00—$159.99 | $18.00 | $600.00—$799.99 | $70.00** |

Cost of items (Order value) _____

Shipping charges (see chart*) _____

TOTAL _____

*Plus, applicable taxes for individuals and other taxable entities (not churches) within Texas will be added. Please call 1-866-249-1799 if the exact amount is needed prior to ordering.

**For order values $800.00 and above, please call 1-866-249-1799 or check www.baptistwaypress.org

Please allow three weeks for standard delivery. For express shipping service: Call 1-866-249-1799 for information on additional charges.

YOUR NAME

PHONE

YOUR CHURCH

DATE ORDERED

SHIPPING ADDRESS

CITY

STATE    ZIP CODE

E-MAIL

**MAIL** this form with your check for the total amount to
BAPTISTWAY PRESS, Baptist General Convention of Texas,
333 North Washington, Dallas, TX 75246-1798
(Make checks to "Baptist Executive Board.")

OR, **FAX** your order anytime to: 214-828-5376, and we will bill you.

OR, **CALL** your order toll-free: 1-866-249-1799
(M-Th 8:30 a.m.-6:00 p.m.; Fri 8:30 a.m.-5:00 p.m. central time),
and we will bill you.

OR, **E-MAIL** your order to our internet e-mail address:
baptistway@bgct.org, and we will bill you.

OR, **ORDER ONLINE** at www.baptistwaypress.org.

We look forward to receiving your order! Thank you!